MW01708505

PROVEN INNOCENCE

PROVEN INNOCENCE

Rick Mehta

Cognitive Psychologist & Defender of Truth

TRUE FREEDOM PRESS

PROVEN INNOCENCE

True Freedom Press's Mission Statement
© 2023 Scott D. G. Ventureyra

Copyright © 2023 Rick Mehta and True Freedom Press. All rights reserved. Except for brief quotations in critical publications or reviews, no part of this book may be reproduced in any manner without permission from the author. Write: Permissions, True Freedom Press, info@truefreedompress.co

Edited by Scott D. G. Ventureyra

First published in Ottawa, Ontario, Canada
in 2023 by True Freedom Press.
https://www.truefreedompress.co
info@truefreedompress.co

If you are interested in publishing with us, please send us an inquiry.

© Cover design conceptualization by Rick Mehta

PAPERBACK ISBN: 978-1-998917-02-0
EBOOK ISBN: 978-1-998917-03-7

Disclaimer Notice

The views and opinions expressed in this book are those of the author and do not necessarily reflect the views or positions of True Freedom Press. It is at Dr. Rick Mehta's discretion to include correspondence between individuals, including the names of certain professors and former students. The editor and publisher disclaim any liability. No part of this book is intended to replace medical, legal, or professional mental help related to any possible topic, subject, issue, or element within this book. Although the editor and publisher have made every effort to ensure that the information in this book was correct at the time of going to press, the editor and publisher do not assume and hereby disclaim any liability to any party for any loss, damage, or disruption caused by error, omissions, negligence, accident, or any other cause.

Table of Contents

Acknowledgements

I extend my heartfelt gratitude to Jesus Christ. Without Him, this book would not have been possible. One of the ways that He works His miracles is by placing the right people in our lives at the right time. In the case of this book, the right person happened to be the editor-in-chief of True Freedom Press: Scott Ventureyra.

As for the timing, in November 2020, I sent Dr. Ventureyra a copy of an article I had written that I had titled "The Campus Culture Wars are Merely a Symptom of a Much Greater Holy War" because I wanted to get his feedback on the ideas that I was communicating. I was pleasantly surprised when he decided to publish that article as a chapter in a book that he edited that was titled *Making Sense Out of Nonsense: Navigating Through the West's Current Quagmire* (2022).

I mention that I was pleasantly surprised by Dr. Ventureyra's reaction because another colleague who read that article warned me that my references to God would harm my credibility in the eyes of free thinkers. This comment suggested to me that many people delude themselves into believing that they are free thinkers when in fact they are slaves to some form of ideology that blinds their minds so that they do not see the treasures that are available only to those who truly believe in Jesus Christ.

Dedication

I dedicate this book to Janice Fiamengo and David Solway. Out of all the people I know, these two have had the biggest influence on how I think. How did they do it? They challenged the beliefs that I had wrongfully cherished.

"Just when I thought I finally learned my lesson well,
there was more to this than meets the eye."

—Bryan Adams/Jim Vallance, "Teacher, Teacher"

True Freedom Press's Mission Statement[1]

True Freedom Press is a unique publishing company that offers editing, design, and writing services and is an alternative press for creative and daring individuals who think freely and for themselves.

To paraphrase a quote commonly attributed to 18th-century French enlightenment philosopher François-Marie Arouet, most commonly known as Voltaire, gets to the essence of what True Freedom Press is all about: "I may not agree with what you say, but I will defend to the death your right to say it." This is exactly why I started True Freedom Press at the end of 2020: to publish books that other presses won't. Even Christian publishing houses would rather appease the world than publish works that defend the truth and God.

Part of the philosophy of True Freedom Press is the recognition that freedom of speech is not only a principle and a basic human right but also a mechanism that has helped democracies survive over the centuries. Free speech has an indispensable functional purpose in facilitating discussion and allowing people to debate uncomfortable ideas while considering differing viewpoints in order to ascertain a better understanding of society and reality. Free speech helps us to sift through good and bad ideas and even expose potentially dangerous and harmful ideas instead of keeping them hidden in the recesses of our minds and on the fringes of society.

True Freedom Press is willing to publish controversial books that challenge established narratives and beliefs and may challenge the beliefs of theists and non-theists. The works published by True Freedom Press may or may not reflect the personal beliefs of the publisher. True Freedom Press is all about publishing books that challenge the status quo. It is a press that supports the pursuit of truth, no matter how uncomfortable, unpopular, or unpleasant it may be to many.

True Freedom Press promotes free speech, freedom of conscience, and freedom of expression. With the pervasiveness of censorship throughout the legacy media, Big Tech platforms such as Facebook, Twitter, Instagram, Google, and others, university campuses, work settings, publishing houses, and even places of worship, true freethinkers are increasingly seeking alternative platforms and methods of communication. True Freedom Press offers an alternative to this Orwellian nightmare that has become so commonplace throughout Western consciousness. It provides a platform for politically correct-averse conservatives,

1 If you're interested in publishing with us, visit us at truefreedompress.co.

theists, libertarians, free thinkers, and others to express their opinions in an open and honest manner.

Little do many realize that political correctness is an oppressive tool to prevent dissenting views. Genocidal tyrants like Mao Zedong used the phrase, which originated with Leon Trotsky. Over the past 20 years, we have seen a dramatic increase in the censorship of unpopular ideas that counter certain narratives, such as woke ideologies, and, in the past three years, anything that counters the single narrative of COVID-19.

True Freedom Press upholds a traditional understanding of tolerance, one that defends an individual's right to hold a particular position and express it freely, even if it offends others. To write freely is to have the ability to offend. The truth may offend at first, but it should be embraced for the sake of authentic living and expression.

Scott D. G. Ventureyra, PhD
Editor-in-Chief at True Freedom Press
Author and editor of *Making Sense of Nonsense*
Ottawa, Canada
July 2023

Preface

> You never really understand a person until you consider things from his point of view, until you climb inside of his skin and walk around in it.
>
> —Harper Lee, *To Kill a Mockingbird*

I worked as a professor in the Department of Psychology at Acadia University between July 1, 2003, and August 31, 2018. On the morning of January 10, 2018, I discovered that the *Chronicle Herald* had published an article about me on the front page of their paper that was titled "Professor Defends Beyak's Remarks," and I knew that my days at the university were numbered. On September 9, 2018, I released a 13-page statement about my dismissal from the university and then responded to a *CBC* journalist's request for an interview. Given that the *CBC* had not interviewed me over the period of January to April 2018, whereas other media outlets had, alarm bells should have gone off in my mind and I should have ignored this interview request. Unfortunately, I made a mistake due to a lapse of judgement.

I was rewarded for my mistake on September 12, 2018, when the *CBC* published an article on their web site that was titled "Controversial Prof Fired for Privacy Breach, Harassment, Acadia Letter Reveals." In that article, the author implied that I had lied in my statement and, as evidence for this allegation, published a discipline letter dated August 3, 2018, instead of my termination letter that was dated August 31, 2018. The letter that the CBC published was then treated as fact by other mainstream media outlets such as *Vice* and went unchallenged by so-called "alternative" or "independent" media outlets such as *True North*, *Rebel Media*, and the *Post Millennial*, as well as by conservative members of Canada's journalistic establishment such as Sue-Ann Levy, Barbara Kay, and Jonathan Kay, all of whom are "selective" about who they choose to defend.[2] Thus, the *CBC* defamed me with their dishonest coverage (an act of commission), whereas the "alternative" or "independent" media defamed me with their silence in the face of an obvious smear campaign by the mainstream media (an act of omission).

2 The comedian and social commentator George Carlin once noted that the establishment is a big club and that ordinary people are not in the club.

Since the publication of the *CBC*'s hit piece, the author (Mairin Prentiss) has become one of my followers on Twitter and is now convinced of my innocence. As well, it was easy for me to forgive her, in part because I understand the mindset that she was in when she wrote her article about me, i.e., I understand the mindset because I am a recovered leftist.

Once I had published *A Service for the People*, I asked myself what my next book project would entail. After giving the issue much thought, I decided to publish this book because I realized that I can prove to a court of public opinion that I had already made enemies with the powers that be at Acadia University before the *Chronicle Herald* published its article about me in January 2018. More importantly, I realized that I can prove to a court of public opinion that I became enemies with them by delivering a talk in which I defended truth. Because I believe that the talk that I delivered is easily my best work, it made sense to publish it so that it can be scrutinized by the public.

The focus of this book is thus on my talk, which I euphemistically refer to as "the big event." However, in order for the reader to understand the context in which I gave my talk, I have also described the major events that transpired in the lead up to "the big event" and in the aftermath of "the big event." The general idea is that I want the public to be able to see the world through my eyes and experience what I experienced by walking a proverbial mile in my shoes. One of my hopes in writing this book is that the public will understand why they should think critically when they are presented with information, especially when that information is from third parties that cannot prove that they are serving the public's interests.

Rick Mehta, PhD
Coldbrook, Nova Scotia
July 2023

Prelude

"The one thing that doesn't abide by majority rule is a person's conscience."

—Harper Lee, *To Kill a Mocking Bird*

June 14, 2017

On May 3, 2017, I hosted a panel discussion that I had organized on the issue of free speech. The event was a resounding success (https://youtu.be/0rRfkDJP_NQ). I received numerous email messages of support from my colleagues for an event that they described as well-planned and informative. Based on the feedback that I had received, I was under the impression that my colleagues were interested in having a discussion about what could and could not be discussed at university campuses and that they were grateful to me for showing leadership.

An interesting fact about the event that I had arranged is that it was supported by Acadia University after I met with Acadia University's Vice-President Academic, Heather Hemming. Specifically, Dr. Hemming's Office gave me a budget of $500 so that I could cover the costs of transportation for the panelists that I had invited and for the cost of a meal for the panelists after the event was over. The mistake that I made at the time was interpreting her Office's financial support for my event as her supporting free speech.

At 3:04 p.m. on Tuesday, June 13, 2017, I received the following email message from Dr. Hemming, which I have copied verbatim.

Hi Rick: I hope you are enjoying this very not day!
I am preparing my report for the Board of Governors and I wanted to share with them the details of the event from May 3rd. Could you send me all of the details that you have and a quote from you about why you took the job on to organize the day and your thoughts on the outcome.
Thank you .
Heather

As soon as I received Dr. Hemming's email message, I started to work on my response because I was keen to meet with her and the incoming president–Dr. Peter J. Ricketts–who was starting his tenure at Acadia University on July 1, 2017. When Dr. Ricketts was a presidential candidate, he stated that he planned on committing the university to social justice. My hope was that he would change his mind if I met with him to discuss the issue. One of the motivations behind the response that I gave to Dr. Hemming was my hope that it would lead to a campus-wide dialogue in which all voices would be heard.

Below is a copy of the email message that I sent to Dr. Hemming at 6:51 p.m. on Wednesday, June 14, 2017:

Hi Heather,

I was glad that you emailed me because I was thinking about contacting Cathy [Dr. Hemming's secretary] about setting up a meeting with you. I've attached my response as a Word document. In this document, I've tried to both give you the information that you need for your report and explain why I want to meet with you. I'll give you a heads up that the document is much longer than what I had intended (apologies in advance for writing a book), but I hope that the information will be helpful in giving you an idea of where I'm coming from.

Thank you,
Rick

And below is a copy of the document that I had attached:

Hi Heather,

Apart from being busy, I hope that all is well at your end. I'm glad that you had emailed me because I was thinking about setting up a meeting with you, but was waiting until I had collected my thoughts a bit more and was in a better position to articulate them. I'll do my best to raise the issues that made me want to meet with you at the end of this message. I'll first address the issues that you'll need for your report to the Board of Governors. I'll address them in separate sections (I hope the headings will be helpful) and will try to give you the details as succinctly as I can. If you need me to expand on or provide references for any of the issues that I've raised, I'd be happy to do so.

I think the easiest place to start, though, is to give you a brief quote that you can use: "The topic of free speech on university campuses has received much coverage in the media and the internet over the past few years, but has received little discussion at our institution. The purpose of this event was to start a dialogue that will build bridges across diverse points of view. My hope is that the discussion that was started on May 3 will continue, both in the Acadia community and at other institutions."

Background Information on Why I Organized the Event

Two events occurred in 2015 that stimulated my interest in the topic of free speech on university campuses. One was an article in Vox by Edward Schlosser (a pseudonym) that was titled "I'm a liberal professor, and my liberal students terrify me," and the other was the protests that took place at Yale University in response to an email that Erika Christakis sent to the students in which she openly disagreed with the administration's position on Halloween costumes.

After a number of other incidents occurred on campuses in Canada and the U.S., I tried to raise this issue at the Fall 2016 Meeting of Faculty, but was told that bringing it to the attention of either AUFA [acronym for my union: Acadia University Faculty Association] or Senate might be more appropriate venues (I can provide the email exchange if you need it). At that time, my impression was that I was the only person on campus interested in the topic of free speech on campuses, so I decided to set the issue aside and not pursue it any further.

Earlier this year, three events happened at around the same time that made me decide that this issue had to be discussed. One was the protests that occurred at McMaster University, in which a panel discussion on free speech – which included Jordan Peterson – was cancelled due to protests (two members of the panel dropped out; Jordan Peterson couldn't talk over the loud volume of the protestors). The second was the cancellation of Danielle Robitaille's talk at Wilfred Laurier because of protests over the fact that she was one of the lawyers who had defended Jian Ghomeshi. The third was the violent protests that occurred at Middlebury College in response to a discussion that included Charles Murray (a co-author of "The Bell Curve") on the panel. In this case, Alison Sanger (I believe she was a member of the panel) suffered from whiplash and a concussion during the protests. Her letter to the New York Times, in which she described her experience and her thoughts on the factors that contributed to the violence, was eye-opening. Another response that stood out for me was the joint statement by Cornel West (a self-described radical Democrat) and Robert George (a prominent conservative intellectual) denouncing what they have termed a climate of "campus illiberalism" at universities. Because there didn't seem to be an obvious route that I could use to discuss these events, I decided to take the lead and organize an event independently.

Details of Panel Discussion

When organizing the panel discussion, I decided to invite Marc Ramsay (Philosophy, Acadia) and Erin Crandall (Politics, Acadia) - based on their views, expertise, and experience. To have a different perspective, I decided to invite two faculty members from other institutions: Mark Mercer (Philosophy, Saint Mary's University) and Steve Perrott (Psychology, Mount Saint Vincent University). Mark Mercer is the president of the Society for Academic Freedom and Scholarship (SAFS) and Steve Perrott is a regular contributor to SAFS's newsletters. Finally, I asked Diane Holmberg (Psychology) to moderate the session based on her extensive experience of having chaired meetings of AUFA [Acadia University Faculty Association] and Senate in a fair and meticulous manner.

When organizing the panel discussion, I first proposed the questions that would be addressed to the members of the panel. When the panel was in agreement, I included these questions in the email messages that I sent to faculty and staff so that the university community could have input into the discussion. The questions ended up being: 1) Is there a problem with free speech on university campuses? 2) If there is a problem, why? In other words, what are some of the underlying causes or contributing factors? and 3) What are potential solutions?

The event was held on Wednesday, May 3 at 10 am in the Auditorium of the KC Irving Centre. The discussion lasted about an hour, and was followed by questions and comments, which lasted for about an hour.[3]

Outcomes

The feedback that I received was far better than I ever expected. When I first publicized the event, I received multiple requests to have the event live-streamed and recorded. I posted the recording on You Tube (https://www.youtube.com/watch?v=0rRfkDJP_NQ) and hope that it will be useful and informative to anyone who watches it.

I also received complimentary emails from colleagues whose views ranged across the political spectrum (e.g., from the die-hard AUFA

3 Because I was being diplomatic, I did not add that I had thought that the people who were opposed to free speech expressed their views in the form of emotional rants that were incomprehensible.

supporters[4] to ones who strongly disagree with AUFA). All of the colleagues who emailed me said that the discussion was informative and that they appreciated hearing very different points of view. For me, an eye-opening moment occurred when Marc Ramsay, who at the outset had argued that there wasn't much of a problem of free speech on campus, admitted that he often self-censors while on campus and was a bit worried about people outside of the university hearing his views on an open letter that was written to the journal Hypatia about an article that was written by Rebecca Tuvel (I'll expand on this issue in the next section).[5]

As a result of this event, some students are planning on holding their own panel discussion in September. Whereas mine was geared towards Acadia's faculty while being open to anyone else, their event will be geared towards students while being open to anyone else who is interested. Since the event, I have heard that some students are interested in being on the panel but are worried that what they say could be held against them in their courses. Some of the students who are on the more conservative side of the political spectrum have told me that they sometimes feel uncomfortable speaking in class because of fear of being ostracized in class, and that they would like to see more political diversity in the speakers that are invited to campus (in other words, they tend to be on the liberal end and that there's little representation from speakers whose views are more conservative or libertarian). As well, one colleague told me that her son (who attends a different university) is sometimes made to feel unwelcome to participate in class discussions because he is male (I believe that being white might have also been a factor, but I'm not 100% certain). I think that we would both agree that these comments are cause for concern.[6]

4 I used the term "die-hard AUFA supporter" instead of "social justice warrior" (SJW) or "obviously mentally ill members of faculty" because I was being diplomatic.

5 I now know why Dr. Ramsay made this contradictory statement: He has long been a grievance officer with the Acadia University Faculty Association. To be in that position, one is required to sign a non-disclosure agreement. The rationale for requiring grievance officers to sign non-disclosure agreements is straightforward: The unions and administrations at unionized workforces want their grievance officers to be in a legal position in which they are unable to disclose the corruption that they witness daily. Unfortunately, people who sign non-disclosure agreements do not realize that these legal documents cannot be used as "get out of jail free" cards when they appear before our Creator and have to account for their actions while they were alive.

6 I had no idea at the time about how mistaken I was in my beliefs when I wrote this sentence.

Incidents Since Free Speech Event

When I organized the panel discussion, I was concerned about issues such as students protesting speakers whose views the students opposed (e.g., Jordan Peterson). Since then, the protests have changed so that faculty and students are attacking people who are on the same side of the political spectrum. In the Tuvel controversy, the author wrote an article in the feminist philosophy journal Hypatia in which she argued that transracialism should be accepted in the same manner that being transgender should be accepted; after this article was published, an open letter was written that demanded that the journal retract the article. Although the editors decided to not retract the article, some have written that the treatment Tuvel received was in line with a witch hunt. The part that stands out to me in this case is that it was faculty who are on the liberal/progressive end of the political spectrum who were attacking themselves.

More recent is the incident that occurred at Evergreen State College. I'm not sure how much you have heard about this incident given that it has received little coverage in the media. Prior to this year, the university had a tradition known as the Day of Absence in which People of Colour would not come to campus for a day. This year, a decision was made to ask white people to not come to campus (although the decision was worded as a friendly request, it was clear that people would be made to feel unwelcome if they didn't comply). Bret Weinstein, a faculty member in Biology, sent an email to the campus community objecting to the request (I can't remember if he also said this part in his email message, but I know that he had voiced concerns about equity playing a key role in future hires). After sending that email message, a group of about 50 students stood outside of his classroom; when he went to talk to them, he was called a racist and the protestors demanded that he resign. Any attempts to reason with the group were futile. After that, he was told that he couldn't hold his classes on campus because the police couldn't guarantee his safety; he ended up holding these classes in a public park. In addition to confronting Bret Weinstein, a group of protestors met with the president of the university (George Bridges). The video footage of the interactions of the protestors with the president was surreal. I'll provide three examples: 1) At one point, he was gesturing the way most people do when talking; that was greeted by calls of "microaggressions" and he was told to stand with his hands at his side; 2) The protestors wouldn't let him go to the washroom by himself; and 3) His request for some personal space because of having claustrophobia was greeted with derision.

Much like the Hypatia controversy, in this incident, students were protesting faculty members and a president who are on the liberal end of the political spectrum. For example, when Bret Weinstein was interviewed by Tucker Carlson on Fox News, Weinstein described himself as someone who is deeply progressive and stated how he voted for Bernie Sanders instead of Hillary Clinton. As well, when he was an undergraduate, he ended up receiving death threats when he stood up against a fraternity for their treatment of black prostitutes. With regard to the university president, George Bridges is a sociologist who has devoted his academic career to advocating for the poor and the disenfranchised. I don't think that any reasonable person would find evidence for Bret Weinstein or George Bridges being racists, but they were treated as if they were bigots.

Implications for Acadia: Concerns and Potential Solutions

This brings me to why I would like to meet with you when you have a moment. These types of incidents have been occurring at universities in Canada and the US, and I think that there is a desire for discussion. So far, we haven't had to deal with any of these controversies at Acadia, but I think that we should be prepared. For example, given the rise of men's issues awareness groups (sometimes called men's rights activists) on other campuses—at this stage, I know of ones at Simon Fraser University, Ryerson University, and the University of Toronto—I think there's a high probability that we will have a group on our campus. If this happened, would we know how we would react? I think a similar argument could be made for pro-life groups.

One problem that has arisen is that university faculty tend to be almost exclusively liberal/progressive. In the past, the ratio of liberal to conservative professors was 2:1. At some institutions, this ratio is as high as 60:1. I don't know what the ratio would be at Acadia. But if we looked at the way that our faculty votes in the NS election, I'd predict that the percentage of people who voted for the NDP and Green parties would be higher than the percentages in the population, and that the percentage of people who voted for the PCs would be substantially lower; I'm not sure what the results would look like for the Liberal party.

This is a concern for me because if the progressive view is pretty much the only view on campus and other voices are not allowed to be heard (e.g., for fear of being called a racist for disagreeing with any component of equity), then there is little to discuss. In this case,

I wouldn't be surprised if the result would become a competition for who is the most progressive, and I don't see how this is productive. In the past, I was reluctant to voice this concern out of fear of being ostracized, but some recent articles in the mainstream media suggest that there is a basis for my concern (from the New York Times: "When the Left Turns on Its Own" and "These Campus Inquisitions Must Stop"; from the Wall Street Journal: "The Campus Mob Came for Me—and You, Professor, Could Be Next").

As well, I think that this would have implications for our enrollment. Every time an incident like the ones I've described occurs at a university and is reported in the media, that gives the impression to prospective students and their parents that only liberal points of view are tolerated. I can't speak for anyone else, but if I were a conservative parent and I was trying to decide what my child should do after high school, I would be extremely reluctant to send them to a university. As well, Conservative Leader Andrew Scheer has already stated that free speech at universities is one of his priorities. If he does end up becoming prime minister, I think this will have implications for our university and curricula.

On the bright side, I also believe that there is a solution. I have come across the Heterodox Academy, which is trying to foster diversity in viewpoints at universities. One of their recommendations is that universities adopt the principles set forth by the University of Chicago last year. I would like to meet with you and/or our incoming president (Peter Ricketts) about adopting these principles. If it is possible for me to get any other relevant parties on board, I would ultimately like this to result in a motion at the May 2018 meeting of the faculty. I also have some ideas of my own that I would like to discuss.

I apologize for this message being much longer than I had anticipated. But I think it has helped me to formulate my thoughts and concerns, and would allow me to articulate myself a bit more clearly when we do have the opportunity to meet in person. I thank you for taking the time to read what I have written and look forward to your response.

Sincerely,
Rick

June 21, 2017

One week after I had responded to Dr. Hemming's email message, I received the following email message from her at 7:50 a.m. on Wednesday, June 21, 2017, which I have copied verbatim:

Hi Rick,
Thank you very much for taking the time to respond to my question with this detailed explanation. Later in the summer I would like to get together with you to discuss it further.

Best,
Heather

July 14, 2017

When a few weeks went by and I did not hear from Dr. Hemming, I decided to show leadership by delivering a talk on the issue of free speech. I was hoping that my act of giving a talk would encourage the administration to change their minds. To give my talk an air of credibility with the student body, I reached out to Sid Kondapuram, editor-in-chief of Acadia University's student newspaper (*The Athenaeum*), and we came up with the following idea: I would deliver a talk that would then be fact-checked by the staff of the newspaper, with the facts then being discussed by a separate independent panel. Mr. Kondapuram informed me that he thought that we would be in a stronger position if we also had the support of the Acadia Students' Union (ASU), and he asked me to write a memo to the president of the ASU, Grace Hamilton-Burge, on his behalf. A key point to keep in mind is that I asked the ASU to **endorse** my talk (bolding is done for emphasis).

Below is a copy of the memo that I wrote for Mr. Kondapuram:

Memo

To: ASU Executive
From: Sid Kondapuram, Editor-in-Chief, The Ath
Date: July 14, 2017

The Ath intends to spur sets of discussions throughout the school year on controversial or interesting topics, with the primary intention of pulling in students and discussing their views in a forum where they are able to articulate them and have them expressed on an equitable standing with faculty. The first of these discussions will be on the topic of *"Free Speech in Universities: Threats and Opportunities."*

Preceding the discussion panel shall be a talk by Dr. Rick Mehta (Department of Psychology, Acadia University). His talk will start with his impressions of what factors are contributing to the problem of suppressed or limited free expression at universities. From there, he will provide support for his supposition by reviewing examples at American and Canadian universities in which students, faculty, and/or administrations have contributed to this problem. In the last part of his talk, he will provide potential solutions that can be discussed by the Acadia community.

To distinguish his talk from other ones that are already on the internet and to raise the bar for academic standards, Dr. Mehta will make his slides available to the public (and of course the panel) after his talk is over. The majority of his slides will have sources (e.g., links to web sites or articles) in the notes section that will be rigorously fact-checked by the staff of The Ath so that students can critically analyze the sources that he used for themselves. The idea here is that he wants what he says to be transparent and easy to scrutinize. As well, to address the criticism that advocates for free speech hold events to speak to people who already agree with them (e.g., the Freedom Summit that was held in Toronto earlier this summer), Dr. Mehta is explicitly stating that he is tailoring this talk for people who disagree with him. As well, he is giving his word that he will not be using any derogatory or inflammatory rhetoric (e.g., terms such as "SJW", "cultural Marxists", etc.).

I anticipate that his talk will take place in the third or fourth week of September and that the discussion panel will take place the following week; the rationale here is that I want to give the Acadia community time to think about and analyze what was said in the talk before discussing the points he raised. If at all possible, The Ath is planning to coordinate the talk and/or panel discussion with the other universities in the Maple League. The panel shall be moderated by a party chosen by The Ath, and all the arrangements for livestreaming, locations, panelists, and advertising etc. shall also be arranged by The Ath.

At this time, we are seeking the ASU's endorsement on holding this event. This would aid in adding legitimacy and also show to the general student populace that the ASU is in support of free speech and open debate on our campus. If you have any questions or concerns, or need more information, please feel free to contact me. I thank you for your time and consideration, and look forward to your response.

July 26, 2017

At 1:08 p.m. on July 26, 2017, I was copied on an email message that ASU President Grace Hamilton-Burge sent to Sid Kondapuram in which she asked what steps we were taking to ensure that there would be no "hate speech" in the events that we were planning. At the time, I was perplexed by her message because I had thought that she meant threats of violence against an individual or group of people when she referred to "hate speech." In hindsight, I now realize that her concern about "hate speech" was an early sign that she makes decisions on the basis of her emotions rather than an objective review of evidence; another warning sign was her statement in which she wrote that the Executive of the Acadia Students' Union "felt"–instead of "thought"– that the free speech panel event that I had organized in May was successful.

Below is a copy of the email message that Ms. Hamilton-Burge sent to Mr. Kondapuram and on which I was copied:

Hello Sid!

In doing my due diligence for supporting this event around free speech I'd like to ask how you are ensuring that all voices can be heard at this event and feel comfortable voicing their opinions. I would also like to ask how you will ensure that the free speech line does not cross into the hate speech line. Perhaps you and Dr. Mehta could let me know the answers to these questions? The Executive Team felt that the event in May was a great and successful event that was well received and respectful.

I think this event will be wonderful and we are really looking forward to promoting it on campus. I hope you both understand that since we are supporting this event we want to not be a part of the planning but part of ensuring that it runs smoothly.

Thank you!
Grace

Below is Mr. Kondapuram's response to Ms. Hamilton-Burge's email message to us; I was not copied on his response:

Hey Grace,

I think we have an adequate number of safeguards for ensuring that panelists don't cross the line into hate speech.

i) The panelists are professors and students from Acadia. This increases accountability for what they discuss in the panel
ii) The questions posed to the aforementioned panelists are from a talk held by Dr. Mehta that will precede the panel. This keeps The Ath in control of the talking points of the panel as every thing presented in the talk is going to be rigorously fact checked by our staff, and we'll ensure that is up to the boundaries of what constitutes hate speech
iii) The panel will be moderated by a candidate of The Ath's choosing. In case that things do get out of hand they will be a party that quickly ensures that no boundary is crossed

As for all the voices being heard, I think that's going to be more about the diversity of the panel. So that we can adequately have people representing the plethora of views on the issue. There will be a (short) question and answer period afterwards, maybe that solves the problem with any individual having an issue with what was said on stage.

Let me know if you want me to flesh out any more of these viewpoints, or have any questions. Hope you're having an incredible time out west!

Cheers,
Sid

At 1:34 pm on July 26, 2017, Ms. Hamilton-Burge emailed Mr. Kondapuram and me to let us know that her concerns had been addressed. Below is a copy of the email message that she sent us:

Hello Sid,

Thank you so much for these answers, they are greatly appreciated! I don't feel the need to flesh out anymore, that all looks wonderful.

Have a wonderful day!
Grace

At that point, I was optimistic that everything would go smoothly with my talk because I had the support of both the student union and student-run newspaper. Little did I know that that support would be short-lived.

September 17, 2017

On September 17, 2017, *The Athenaeum* published an article on its web site that was written by Emi Vagatoth. For this article, Ms. Vagatoth interviewed me to ask me about the talk that I was going to be delivering on September 27. I became suspicious of Mr. Kondapuram when I noticed that he had published her article only on *The Athenaeum's* web site, which few students access. In other words, this article was not published in the hard copies of the student newspaper that are widely distributed on campus and was not posted on any of the newspaper's social media platforms that students use to share information.

In terms of how to proceed with the issue of reproducing this article in *Proven Innocence*, I reached out to *The Athenaeum* and to Mr. Jack Graham (counsel, Acadia University) to ask them if I needed permission from Acadia University or any of its subsidiaries in order to reproduce the student newspaper's article in this book, and to let me know what procedures I must follow in case I do need their permission. I also asked them why the author is now listed as "athphoto" instead of Emi Vagatoth.

Because I have not received a response from the parties, much less one in which I have been told that I need Acadia University's permission to reproduce an article that was written about me that depicted me truthfully, I have reproduced the article below, which I retrieved from https://theath.ca/science/dr-rick-mehta-teaching-style-research-thoughts-free-speech/:

Dr. Rick Mehta on his Teaching Style, Research and Thoughts on Free Speech

By athphoto | Published September 17, 2017

Dr. Rick Mehta is well-known on the Acadia campus for teaching Acadia's biggest course, Introductory Psychology, but also for being a friendly and active member of the Acadia community. He can often be found going on a run around campus or singing in the Acadia University Chorus. In light of Dr. Mehta's upcoming talk on "Free Speech in Universities: Threats and Opportunities", I sat down with him to get some insight into his research interests, teaching style and thoughts on issues university students are facing today.

Dr. Mehta began his post-secondary education with his B.Sc. at the University of Toronto in Scarborough from 1989 to 1993. He debated doing a biology and psychology double major but settled instead on a neuroscience degree which he felt was the best of both worlds. From 1994 to 1996, he did his M.Sc. in psychopharmacology at McGill University to study the effects of drugs on rats' brains. This was challenging due to a very uncomfortable allergy to rats and so he then switched to studying how people learn about correlations between events (and their role in decision making) as his Ph.D. project at McGill. After completing a three year Post-Doctoral Fellowship at the University of Winnipeg, Dr. Mehta came to Acadia in 2003.

When asked about what he finds special about Acadia, he remarked at how, even being in a class in Acadia's biggest classroom, Huggins 10, one can still feel a sense of community with those around you. This sense of community and belonging in a group appeals to him and, along with the pure joy of creating music, is the reason why he takes part in the Acadia chorus. He enjoys this opportunity to be equals with his students and to interact with them as peers rather than as a professor standing in front of them in a classroom.

Introductory Psychology is a course that many students find themselves taking at one point throughout their Acadia career, and Dr. Mehta's teaching of it has helped to make it quite popular. He always arrives a few minutes early to chat with students and plays a song at the beginning of every class. To him, the necessary formula of a good lecture incorporates content that is both accessible and structured above all else but woven as much as possible with breaks for humour.[7] Indeed, when I asked him if there was someone he'd encountered throughout his career who'd inspired him to teach in the unique style he's adopted, his answer was to show me his forearms. Tattooed on his arms, are the faces of Rush band members. He explained to me that he tries to integrate what Rush does in their music and concerts into his teaching. The band member Neil Peart is the serious one in the group who writes the lyrics, while Geddy Lee adds structure and Alex Lifeson infuses humour and improvisation into Rush's songs and concerts. To Dr. Mehta, these are the three most important elements he wants to incorporate into his teaching. Like Rush, he has something serious to share but wants to deliver it with as much joy and accessibility as possible.

Dr. Mehta's research interests lie in the field of decision making. Recently, he's been looking into the role of various predictors that play a role in decision making tasks. One predictor that he described was the Cognitive Reflection Test. This is a test where a question may be worded such that there seems to be an intuitive answer but it's actually incorrect. An example question looks like this: "A bat and a ball cost $1.10 in total. The bat costs a $1.00 more than the ball. How much does the ball

7 The point that I was hoping to communicate is that I take issues seriously but that I don't take myself seriously.

cost?" Many people would say ¢10 whereas if you really think about it, the answer is ¢5. Recent research suggests that low scores on this task are associated with real-life outcomes such as increased credit card debt and failing to secure our computers (e.g., not being careful about our privacy settings when using social media).

Other predictors he has studied include the ways people process information, how much they enjoy being challenged, how much faith they put into intuition and how they reason with numbers in relation to decision making. These types of studies are relevant because there are plenty of everyday examples where quick decision making is necessary but can have consequences on a person's well-being. For example, nutrition labels are supposed to be easily accessible to the public, and yet his research group has found that complex numerical and reading comprehension skills are actually needed to fully understand them.

I asked him if he had any advice to share with students who may be interested in also pursuing a career in research and his advice was to follow your strengths and to think creatively about your options. While the high level of competition for research jobs in the academic context may make a career in research seem daunting, there are plenty of alternative places to look to gain interesting experience. For example, research jobs in the private industry, government or military may have less competition and be just as interesting and rewarding.

Since Dr. Mehta's upcoming talk on free speech has been a highly controversial topic in universities in Canada and the United States, I asked him for a preview of his stance and objectives in giving it. I learned that his goal is to address a persisting issue and to provide an outlet for a discussion that avoids setting off a rally or further polarization of viewpoints. He plans to provide evidence of a growing lack of civil discourse in universities and so a polarization of viewpoints leading to a new kind of discrimination. As he put it, "throughout human history, people have had a tendency to separate ourselves into us versus them groups, and the growing trend now is for people to discriminate against each other based on their views or ideas."

His hope in giving this talk is to reach out to people who disagree with him so as to be able to follow up his talk later with a well-rounded panel discussion that has the potential to start a conversation within the university community. He plans to bring evidence from studies and incidents on Canadian and American University campuses to discuss how to approach this challenging subject. He feels that suppressing hate speech will not be the most effective way to eliminate hate and will bring ideas for how else to address this problem. He plans to discuss the shift in political ideologies on campuses across Canada that have inadvertently shifted to become disconnected with the rest of society. His concern with this being, that if viewpoints go very far in one direction, it can lead to a polarization that creates a rebellion for polarization in the opposite direction. This issue and debate exists in university campuses across North America, and if you can't talk about it in university, then where can you talk about it?

To hear more about Dr. Mehta's impressions of the factors affecting free speech in universities, join him for his talk "Free Speech in Universities: Threats and Opportunities" from 7 to 8:30pm in BAC 132 on September 27th, 2017.

September 25, 2017

Because I was concerned about protests at my upcoming talk, I decided to circulate an email message to all faculty and staff at Acadia University so that I could address the rationale for why people would protest my talk. I also copied Mr. Kondapuram (editor-in-chief of The Athenaeum) and Ms. Hamilton-Burge (President of Acadia's Student Union) on this message. One of the key points that I will highlight is that my overall concern was that I was living in a society in which people were losing their humanity. Below is a copy of the email message that I circulated at 12:17 p.m. on Monday, September 25, 2017:

Good Afternoon Acadia Community,

As you may already be aware, I'll be giving a talk titled "Free Speech in Universities: Threats and Opportunities" on Wednesday at 7 p.m. in BAC 132. The purpose of this message is to alleviate any potential concerns that my talk is in any way advocating for or endorsing hate speech. Rather, the purpose of the talk is to address the broad issue of censorship that's taking place in society, with the university campuses being part of the bigger picture. As shown in the outline for the talk that I have included later in this email message, I will address the issue of hate speech early in my talk.

Unlike other events on free speech that have been held at universities (e.g., the Free Speech Summit that took place in Toronto this past summer), my intended audience is not going to be people who already agree with me. Instead, my target audience will be people who are on the fence or who even vehemently disagree with me on this now controversial issue. The ultimate goal of this talk will be to get conversations started on campus about broad/general issues related to free speech and to have a plan in place that will lead to specific policy proposals that I can submit to either the Senate or Faculty in 2018.

One key argument that I'll be making is that we're now living in an age where we are using viewpoints as a way of separating people into us versus them. The implication of doing so is that we treat others who have a different point of view as being sub-human and, in the process of doing so, risk losing our humanity in the process. As evidence, I'll be describing the actions of people on the extreme left and the extreme right ends of the political spectrum within the university context. Finally, I'll make the argument that universities now have the opportunity (I wonder if duty is not too strong a word) to be the voice of reason during these polarized times.

With regard to the email message I sent to Acadia-FYI over the weekend, I have made arrangements to ensure that the talk will be recorded. This way, people who cannot attend the talk will be able to watch it once it is available on places such as YouTube. I will also make my slides available to the university community and the general public. I will also make available a list of sources that went into the talk. At this stage, my reference section is 19 pages long and still growing, and this is without using formats such as APA or MLA, which would make this section even longer. The purpose behind these actions is to give the university community and general public as much information as they need so that they can fact-check and scrutinize every word that I am saying for themselves. In other words, I do not expect anyone to take any of my arguments at face value because that goes against the university's goal of encouraging and developing critical thinking and evidence-based decision-making.

Below is the outline for my talk:

- Reasons for Supporting Free Speech
- Addressing Hate Speech
- Examples of Suppression of Free Speech
  - England
  - US
  - Canada
- Contributing Factors
- Evergreen State College
- Potential Solutions
  - Addressing hate
  - Acadia taking action

As you can see, I will be covering a lot of ground during the talk. Given this, I anticipate that my talk will be roughly 1 hour and 15 minutes, which is longer than the norm of 45 minutes and then time for questions. The posters that have been used to advertise this talk have allotted 90 minutes for the event. However, my understanding is that I'll still have the room available after 8:30, which means that there will still be ample time for questions and discussion after the talk is over.

Please feel free to email me if you need more information, or have either questions or concerns. I look forward to seeing whoever can make it and to discussing this issue further over the remainder of the academic year.

Sincerely,
Rick

The next section of this book contains a "transcript" of my talk, "Free Speech in Universities: Threats and Opportunities." I used quotation marks around the word "transcript" because, rather than being a word-for-word reproduction of what I said that night, the next section consists of a faithful reproduction of what I had said. To accomplish this goal, I asked Dr. Ventureyra to draft a transcript in which he removed common fillers that speakers unconsciously use when they deliver lectures, such as "um" and "basically." He also fixed minor grammatical errors and errors in sentence structure that are acceptable in speech but stand out like sore thumbs in written text. I then further polished the text by removing redundancies and organizing the "transcript" into paragraphs. Finally, I added commentary in the footnotes about the sections of my talk that I think have aged well and those that have not. I hope that the written version of my talk will be as clear as the verbal version that I delivered.

The Big Event

Free Speech in Universities: Threats and Opportunities

Rick Mehta
Department of Psychology
Acadia University

"When perspectives are unrepresented in discussions, when some kinds of thinkers aren't at the table, classrooms become echo chambers rather than sounding boards — and we all lose."
- Nick Kristof

Universities have traditionally been venues in which ideas can be freely exchanged. The underlying assumption has been that any idea, regardless of how controversial it is, can be discussed and scrutinized in an academic setting. By using tools such as discussion and debate, as well as data analysis and interpretation, poor ideas are debunked and discredited while ideas with merit flourish. The notion has been that society benefits from adopting ideas that have been rigorously vetted as opposed to adopting ideas that may well be mainstream and widely accepted but are still incorrect and wrong. As the saying goes, "Just because everyone says something doesn't mean it's true."

This whole process is based on the principle of free speech, the notion that any idea—no matter how offensive or subversive it may be to mainstream society—can be expressed and discussed in an institution of higher learning.

Reasons for Supporting Free Speech

- How do we acquire knowledge about issues or have the capacity to solve difficult problems if we cannot talk about them?
- Speech codes work against the interests of neurodiversity
- Antifragility
- Discomfort often a component of change
- Allowing the expression of offensive speech may actually play a role in positive social change

There are five reasons why I am arguing for this position. The first reason has to do with the question, "How do we acquire knowledge about issues or have the capacity to solve problems if we cannot talk about them?" To quote from John Stuart Mill: "He who knows only his own side of the case knows little of that. His reasons may be good, and no one may have been able to refute them. But if he is equally unable to refute the reasons on the opposite side, if he does not so much as know what they are, he has no ground for preferring either opinion."

I will give you an example of a friend of mine, Paul Mackenzie, when he was an undergraduate: In one of his classes, the students debated about whether or not women should get to vote, and he had the thankless task of being on the side favouring the idea that women do not get to vote. Clearly, this is a very distasteful position to have to argue in favour of.[8] But, afterwards, he said he was better able to articulate why it is that women should be able to vote because you have to think of the other side, and that made him better able to articulate exactly why that is. So, that is one reason we ought to look at a side, even if it is offensive.

The second argument that I'll mention is that Geoffrey Miller argues that the use of speech codes and other techniques to suppress free speech works against the interests of neurodiversity. What "neurodiversity" refers to are people who have conditions such as autism spectrum disorder, bipolar disorder, or Tourette's Syndrome. The way their brain is organized is different than a typical brain, and the premise here is that when we use speech codes, we're imposing the rules of

8 Statements such as this one show that there was a liberal bias in my talk, even though I did my best to not be biased. My current stance is that liberals and conservatives are different wings of the same nut. My reasoning is straightforward: the political left vs. right debate is rooted in dishonesty because rights and responsibilities go hand in hand. In other words, it is dishonest to argue for one (e.g., rights) without also taking into consideration the other (e.g., responsibility).

a typical brain onto people who have a neurodiverse brain. So the argument he makes is: "How can we make the case that we are inclusive, as a university, if we start imposing speech codes against those who are not neurotypical?"

The third is the notion of "antifragility." Jonathan Haidt, in his talks known on YouTube as "Truth University vs. Social Justice University" and "Coddling University versus Strengthening University," argues against the notion of universities being safe spaces. Instead, he argues for the principle known as "antifragility"—the notion that short-term exposure to ideas that make us uncomfortable in the short term actually makes us stronger in the long term. This is analogous to how our immune system works when we have vaccinations[9] or how we build muscle. The idea is that these systems work precisely because they are challenged.

I would take this notion a step further and say that discomfort is a key component of any meaningful change. From the health psychology literature, we know that lifestyle changes often occur only after people reach a tipping point where they are no longer comfortable with their circumstances and decide to make changes, such as adopting healthier eating habits, quitting smoking, or exercising. We can also argue that this applies to social change. People are uncomfortable with their situation and say they've had enough, and this is what instigates change.

In a couple of minutes, I will argue for something that will probably be very counterintuitive to many people, which is that allowing people to express views that are offensive may actually play a role in instigating positive social change.

9 At the time, I did not know that vaccinations are a scam.

Addressing Hate Speech

- Canada already has hate speech laws
- Suppressing hate speech does not suppress hate
- Who gets to decide which views can and cannot be expressed?

Before we get to that, I thought I'd turn briefly to the issue of hate speech because I received numerous requests to address it.

One issue is that Canada already has hate speech laws.[10] According to the lawyer John Carpay, who founded the Justice Centre for Constitutional Freedoms, Canada already has healthy boundaries that make it illegal for any person to call for another person or group of people to be harmed in any way, which include robbery, assault, having their homes burned, or being killed. Because these protections are already in place, Carpay argues that universities should be safe spaces from assault or harm but not from ideas that make people upset; they get upset mostly because they disagree with the ideas or find them offensive.[11]

In terms of a related talk, I would recommend the talk by Christina Brehm, who talks about her experiences in East Germany after World War II.

The third argument is that it's easy for people who are in power to say, "I have concerns, and that's why it is okay for me to tell you not to speak." But the issue that raises itself is: "Who should get to decide whose views can and cannot be expressed?"

10 A point that I should have mentioned is that this is in contrast to the United States, where "hate speech" is considered protected speech thanks to the First Amendment in that country's constitution.

11 From their actions, it is clear that the Justice Centre for Constitutional Freedoms is not opposed to "hate speech" legislation. In contrast, I now take the position that "hate speech" legislation needs to be struck down as unconstitutional.

MACLEAN'S

AUTHORS WATCH OUR VIDEOS EDUCATION HUB OUR ARCHIVES THE CANADA PROJECT CONTACT US

When science goes silent

With the muzzling of scientists, Harper's obsession with controlling the message verges on the Orwellian

Jonathon Gatehouse

May 3, 2013

Chris Wattie/Reuters

CBCnews | Politics

Home Opinion World Canada Politics Business Health Entertainment Technology & Science Video

Politics Power & Politics CBC SecureDrop

Revenue Canada targets birdwatchers for political activity

Canada Revenue Agency issues warning letter to wildlife club to curb any political activities

By Dean Beeby, CBC News Posted: Oct 16, 2014 5:06 PM ET | Last Updated: Oct 17, 2014 3:03 PM ET

Watching the birdwatchers 2:07

A small group of nature lovers in southern Ontario enjoy spending weekends watching birds and other wildlife, but lately they're the ones under watch — by the Canada Revenue Agency.

It was not that long ago that we were living in the age of Harper's Conservatives, and we heard day in and day out about the muzzling of scientists. Harper's administration went to extreme lengths to silence anyone who said anything against his administration's stance on the environment, including these bird watchers; they made some posters about the environment, and so Revenue Canada came after them.

I just want to make sure that we are all on the same page. When I use the example of the Harper Conservatives, one of their tactics was to say that "this issue is not for debate". Do we agree that that is an unacceptable tactic? [The audience nodded in agreement.] If we agree that it's unacceptable for the Harper Conservatives to conduct themselves this way, then we should agree that it's unacceptable for anyone else in power to act this way.

After a 13-year battle, former Health Canada scientist won't get his job back

The Federal Court of Appeal won't hear the case of a former Health Canada scientist fired for alleged insubordination in 2004.

JOANNE LAUCIUS, OTTAWA CITIZEN

More from Joanne Laucius, Ottawa Citizen

Published on: September 6, 2017 | Last Updated: September 6, 2017 5:56 PM EDT

If we want to go further back in time, for those who remember the early 1990s and 2000s, there was a scientist by the name of Shiv Chopra, and throughout the 1990s he gave the Liberal Government of Jean Chretien and Paul Martin a very difficult time with issues related to our food supply.[12] For example, he argued against certain hormones being used in our milk supply. In 2014, he and three other scientists wrote to Minister Anne McLellan, saying that we should not be using rendered meat to feed cows because that was going to increase the risk of bovine spongiform encephalopathy (mad cow disease). Those scientists ended up getting fired for that. Later, one of them passed away, and two others were reinstated. Thirteen years later, the one person who was most vocal (Dr. Chopra) is still fighting to get his job back. That's across three administrations now: the Martin government that fired him, the Harper government that would not reinstate him, and presently continuing with the Trudeau government.[13]

12 In this section of my talk, I was trying to raise, but not get sidetracked by, the issue of genetically modified organisms (GMOs). Little did I know at the time about the connection between vaccines and GMOs and their implications for Canadians' health.

13 Sadly, Dr. Chopra died in January 2018 and never received the justice that he sought and deserved.

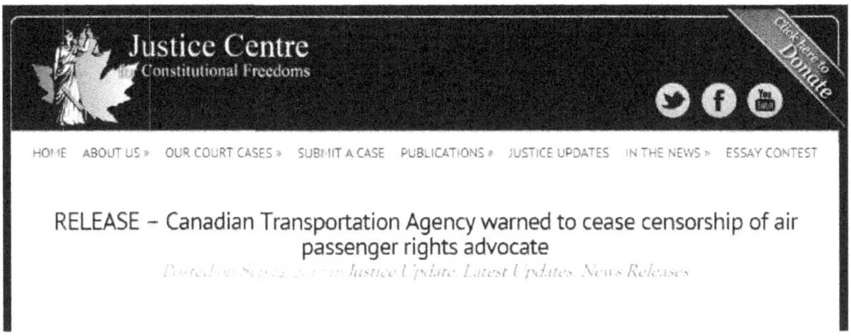

There was a recent case with the "Air Passenger Rights Network," which is headed by Dr. Gábor Lukács. Dr. Lukács published an article titled "Five Reasons Not to Trust the Canadian Transport Agency." He received two private messages over Facebook telling him to remove that message. The Justice Centre for Constitutional Freedoms is now taking up his case.

Clearly, I could go on for ages, but unless we could decide who it should be, it's probably best to argue that no one should have that ability to silence since no one is above the law, i.e., declaring by fiat what is or isn't up for debate. This is happening under the Trudeau government. For now, all I will say is that there are dark clouds behind his "sunny ways."

I want to introduce you to Ruth Simmons. She was born in 1945 in Grapeland, Texas. She was the youngest of 12 children. One thing to note about her is that her great grandparents were slaves. She grew up in poverty during the Jim Crow era of racial segregation. Despite these challenging circumstances, she achieved the top grades in her school and kept receiving award after award. She received her PhD in French literature from Harvard University.

In 1995, she was the first African American president of Smith College, which is a women's college in the US. In her role as president, she started an engineering program and a finance program. Her rationale was that she wanted women to have access to the same high paying jobs as men.

In 2000, she was appointed the first African American president of an Ivy League university: Brown University. She started this position in late 2001. Now, I ask you to put yourself in her shoes in terms of what happened when she got to the institution. She's a descendant of slaves, and as she's walking throughout the institution, on the walls there are pictures of former slave owners; that's one aspect. Also, before she arrived, there was a major controversy. In March 2001, a writer by the name of David Horowitz[14] paid for a full-page advertisement in the student newspaper that was titled "Ten Reasons Why Reparations for

14 I apologize to David Horowitz for mischaracterizing him in my lecture.

Slavery Are a Bad Idea and Racist Too." The argument behind it was that slavery was a non-issue because it happened so long ago, that white Christians had ended it, and that black Americans should be grateful for all the prosperity and freedom they had in the U.S. I hope that you are in agreement with me that these claims are offensive.[15]

But do you know how President Simmons handled that? She insisted that he come back to speak. She attended and sat in the front row. Let's fast forward to 2004, when she appointed a committee on slavery and justice to figure out how to deal with the institution's dark past. She wanted to do it in a way that all points of view could be expressed. She wanted the problem to be solved without endless grievances happening after the fact. I would argue that allowing David Horowitz to speak gave her credibility because people knew that they could express their views and not be tarnished for it.

I want to read some sections from a speech she gave in 2014 at Smith College in which she reflects on her life experiences. I think what she said might have more applicability now than even back in 2014. The first snippet:

> My coming of age was marred by the wide acceptance of the violent suppression of speech. Any criticism or complaint that was deemed unsuitable could result in summary violence against one's family and against one's person. No forums of open expression existed for me or mine in the Jim Crow south of my early youth. Once you have tasted the bitterness and brutality of being silenced in this way, it is easy to recognize the danger of undermining free speech. Our founders began with a lofty ideal, holding certain truths to be self-evident. Little is self-evident in the public space today. Disagreement abounds on every slight and significant matter. Protecting free speech brilliantly insulates us from being silenced from our unpopular views.

Now, the second part:

> One's voice grows stronger in encounters with opposing views. My first year after leaving Smith, I had to insist that Brown permit a speaker whose every assertion was dangerous and deeply offensive to me on a personal level. Indeed, he maintained that blacks were better off having been enslaved.[16] Attending his talk and hearing his perspective was personally challenging but not in the least challenging to my convictions

15 I now regret that I made this statement.

16 This statement is false because it misrepresents David Horowitz, but I did not recognize its falsehood when I delivered my lecture because I still had an unconscious ideological blind spot at the time. The take-home lesson is that ideologies blind people to the truth.

> about the absolute necessity of permitting others to hear him say these heinous things. I could have avoided the talk as his ideas were known to me, but to have done so would have been to choose personal comfort over a freedom whose value is so great to my own freedoms that hearing his unwelcome message could hardly be assessed as too great a cost.[17]

The third snippet:

> Universities have a special obligation to protect free speech, open discourse and the value of protest. The collision of views and ideologies is in the DNA of the academic enterprise.

17 I would now describe this section of her speech as virtue-signalling.

Overview

- Examples of Suppression of Free Speech
  - England
  - US
  - Canada
- Contributing Factors
- Evergreen State College
- Potential Solutions
  - Addressing hate
  - Acadia taking action

While the DNA may not have changed at the level of the genotype, we are seeing—through an epigenetic-like mechanism—a change at the level of the phenotype. What I'll be doing from here is going through examples that have occurred over the last year alone, including examples of the suppression of free speech in England,[18] the U.S., and Canada. I will then go to some of the contributing factors. And I'll take up the case of Evergreen State College because, unless we make a change soon, we are going in a direction where we are going to have the same kind of occurrences happening here in Acadia. From there, I'll address solutions that we can adopt at Acadia.

18 I decided to include England in this lecture for two reasons. The first was to demonstrate that what I was observing in Canada and the US was also happening overseas and therefore was a global phenomenon. The second was that Dr. Peter Ricketts (President, Acadia University) is from Britain, and I was hoping that I could reach him if I talked about his home country in my lecture.

England

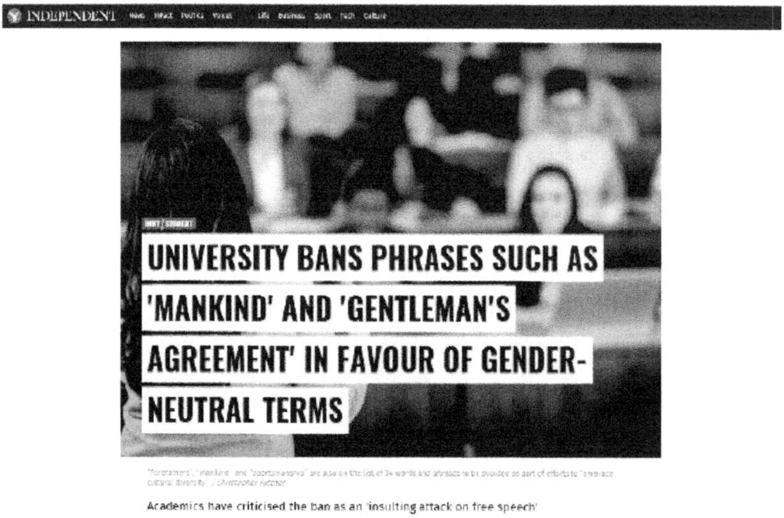
INDEPENDENT

UNIVERSITY BANS PHRASES SUCH AS 'MANKIND' AND 'GENTLEMAN'S AGREEMENT' IN FAVOUR OF GENDER-NEUTRAL TERMS

Academics have criticised the ban as an 'insulting attack on free speech'

In England, some universities are mandating that students use gender-neutral terms. Making something mandatory does not bring out the best in us. To the contrary, Joanna Williams is a professor who argues that all this does is violate academic freedom.

England

theguardian

home › UK › media society law scotland wales northern ireland education

National newspapers

City University students vote for campus ban on Sun, Mail and Express

Student union at university known for its journalism school votes to ban the newspapers in 'opposing fascism' motion

16,059

Mark Sweney and Jasper Jackson

The Telegraph

Education

HOME NEWS SPORT BUSINESS

Primary Secondary University Student life Apprenticeships League tables Professional courses Cl

Education

Whooping should be banned beause it excludes deaf people, Nation Union of Students say

Share 32 Comments

Malia Bouattia is the outgoing NUS president CREDIT: MARK KERRISON / ALAMY STOCK PHOTO

By **Camilla Turner**, EDUCATION EDITOR

27 APRIL 2017 • 8:35PM

Students who whoop, cheer and clap should face "consequences" because they are excluding deaf people, delegates at the National Union of Students conference said.

Other universities are banning certain newspapers on the basis that ideas with which they disagree are "fake news." I'll let this speak for itself.

There's one student group that's arguing that we should not do any cheering or whooping because that's dangerous to deaf people. In the bigger picture, what is happening in England with the Theresa May government is that her funding cuts, including those in health care, are disproportionately affecting young children and the elderly, who are the most vulnerable in our society. She hadn't changed the building code laws, which were thought to have played a role in a fire that killed people in a poor neighbourhood. As well, there were cuts to police services, which were thought to have played a role in some of the incidents of terrorism that have risen. Taking into consideration the major issues that need to be solved, one wonders what the students are thinking when they consider this [the coddling of deaf people] their "cause du jour."

USA

- Pitzer College
- Middlebury College
- University of California, Berkeley

Turning to North America, it is interesting to see the interplay of what is happening on both the extreme left and the extreme right sides of the political spectrum.

At Pitzer College, a resident assistant decided to send out an email to all students in which she argued that white girls should not wear hoop earrings because this is cultural appropriation of black culture. I can relate this to incidents that have happened in Canada. Nikki Ashton (a Member of Parliament) posted a Beyoncé meme saying "to the left," and then she said in her Twitter post—in line with environmental, social, and economic social justice causes— "let's be like Beyonce and go to the left." She then received tweets from Black Lives Matter saying that this was cultural appropriation, and she ended up taking down her comments. The problem with a notion like cultural appropriation is that it is used so widely that, at this point, it loses its meaning, even though it may have had a good meaning to start with.

Most recently, there has been the incident at Middlebury College where Alison Sanger agreed to be on a panel with Charles Murray (a controversial speaker), and there the incident got so out of hand that she ended up in a neck brace due to whiplash and also a concussion.

Then, of course, there is the recent incident at the University of California at Berkeley. At the Milo Yiannopoulos talk, things got so out of hand that there were bricks thrown, fires, and a lot of property damage—about a hundred thousand dollars worth of damage. We are very fortunate that no one was killed in the incident.

To the people who asked me to address the issue of hate speech—I really wish that they would denounce violence from groups like Antifa that claim to be "anti-fascist." [19]

19 I strongly suspect that this comment did not go over well with my detractors at Acadia University.

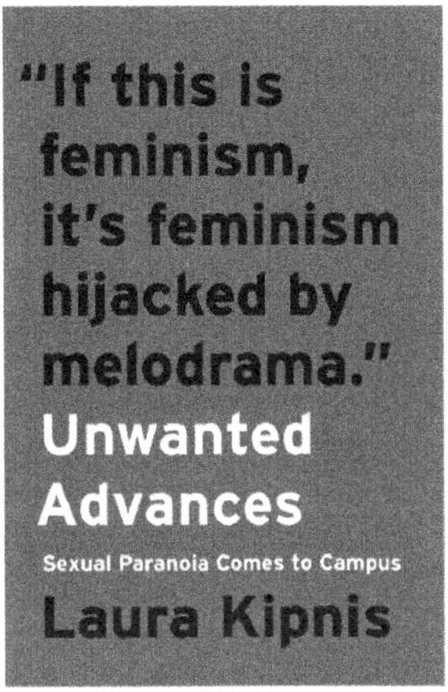

The case I will turn to next is that of Laura Kipnis. What is interesting about her case is that there does not seem to be any rhyme or reason for what is happening here; it is just people attacking each other. I'll give you some background on Kipnis. She's a cultural critic and film professor. She's been labeled a provocative feminist by *The Nation*, a leading liberal magazine. On February 20, 2015, Kipniss published an article in *The Chronicle of Higher Learning* called "Sexual Paranoia Strikes Academe." In that article, she argued that there were problems with Title 9. In the U.S., they have a law called Title 9, which puts a ban on sexual discrimination in educational settings. She argued that Title 9 was being used to intrude into the personal lives of faculty and students. After having written that article, she found herself the target of a Title 9 investigation, the basis being that her article created a climate of fear on campus. She was eventually declared innocent of those charges. After publishing a book titled "Unwanted Advances: Sexual Paranoia Comes to Campus," she went through another Title 9 investigation for sexual harassment.

Oftentimes, when you talk about free speech, it's argued that it's just people who are right-wing trying to argue for their case. To show that this is false, I'm going to read a couple of snippets from her book, *Unwanted Advances* (pages 140–141):

> The reality is that the more [universities] devote themselves to creating "safe spaces," that new campus watchword, the more dangerous campuses have become for professors, and the less education itself

> becomes anyone's priority... Let me just say that nearly every academic I know—this includes feminists, progressives, minorities, and those who identify as gay or queer—now lives in fear of some classroom incident spiralling into professional disaster.
>
> Professors, even at major research universities, now routinely avoid discussing subjects in class that might raise hackles. A well-known sociologist told me that he no longer lectures on abortion. I spoke to an Ivy League law professor whose students won't attend lectures about rape law. Someone who's written a book about incest in her own family described being confronted in class by a student furious with her for discussing the book. A tenured female professor on my campus wrote about lying awake at night worrying that some stray remark of hers might lead to student complaints, social media campaigns, and eventual job loss.

The idea here is not right vs. left or left vs. right; the bigger issue is intolerance. I've focused a bit on the left side of the political spectrum, but we are also seeing some interesting developments from the right side.

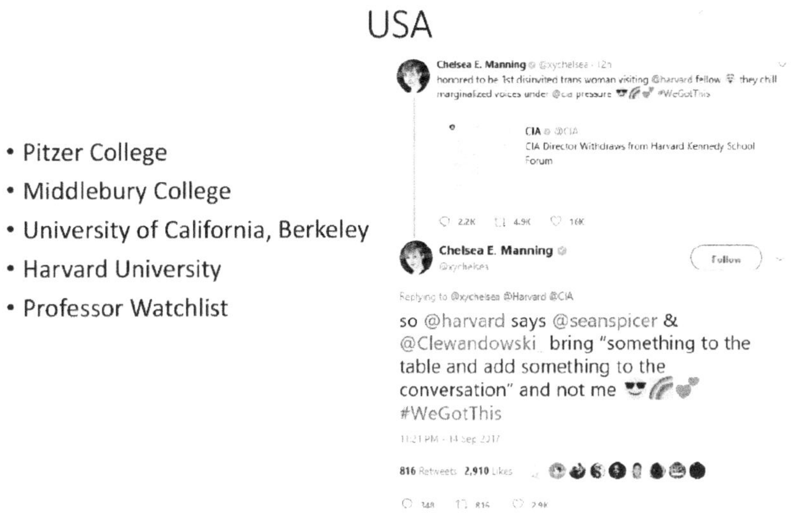

A recent case is that of Chelsea Manning at Harvard University, where she was invited to be a visiting fellow and to come in for a day or two to give some talks. After the invitation was made public, there were denunciations from people within the CIA as well as resignations on campus. Harvard then rescinded their invitation; the tweets in the slide speak to this issue.

This is what I think has happened: With the suppression of free speech on the left side of the political spectrum, those on the right have developed their own methods of retaliation. One method that has been developed is a website named "Professor Watchlist" that denounces liberal professors. Some have argued that it's a "star chamber" that is being used to target liberal professors.[20]

A more recent trend that has happened on the right side of the spectrum is that they'll go after left leaning professors based on their media tweets and Facebook posts. Once the posts are public, magazines such as *Campus Reform* and the *College Fix* report on these incidents, where people on the right side of the spectrum become irate and call for resignations or make death threats.[21] Sometimes the universities capitulate and let them go. This is bad for free speech. Sometimes they are allowed to stay, but this creates a different kind of bitterness.

20 When I delivered my talk, I should have mentioned that others could view this web site as exposing corruption.

21 In retrospect, I could have done a better job of covering the distinction between exposing corruption and people's reactions to corruption. There's nothing wrong with exposing corruption, but one would be hard-pressed to find an argument that justifies calls for death, especially in this context.

USA: Trinity College

Johnny Eric Williams
June 18 at 9:27pm

It is past time for the racially oppressed to do what people who believe themselves to be 'white' will not do, put end to the vectors of their destructive mythology of whiteness and their white supremacy system. #LetThemFuckingDie

Johnny Eric Williams
June 18 at 9:36pm

I'm fed the fuck up with self identified 'white's' daily violence directed at immigrants, Muslim, and sexual and racially oppressed people. The time is now to confront these inhuman assholes and end this now.

CAMPUS REFORM

MEDIAITE

TV OPINION WEIRD TRUMP SPORTS ENTERTAINMENT FOOD NEWSLETTER

283

College Reinstates Professor Who Said To Let White People 'F***ing Die'

by Joe Bilello | 3:47 pm, August 2nd, 2017

Tweet Share reddit

Following the shooting at a Congressional baseball practice in Alexandria, VA back in June, a professor at Trinity College in Connecticut seemed to support the idea that first responders should have let the victims "fucking die" because they were white.

Here is an example of what happened at Trinity College: A professor by the name of Johnny Eric Williams wrote messages on social media in which he made reference to racial issues involving law enforcement and their connection to an officer's fatal shooting of a black woman in Seattle. In one of those posts, he also shared an article by an anonymous author called "Let Them Fucking Die." The article suggested that emergency personnel should have allowed the wounded victims of a congressional shooting incident to die.

I'll give you an idea of what was in that article:

"If you see them drowning. If you see them in a burning building. If they are bleeding out in an emergency room. If the ground is crumbling beneath them. If they are in a park and they turn their weapons on each other: do nothing."

It continues like this for a while and ends with: "Let. Them. Fucking. Die. And smile a bit when you do."

That is the nature of the post that he made. This gives you an idea of what his posts looked like. He received death threats and left town. Eventually, the university decided to reinstate him while also stating that what he posted was despicable.

Unsurprisingly, those on the right side of the political spectrum are asking "What if that had been a white person? Would he still be here?"

We are clearly witnessing a circle of viciousness.

ePaper NATIONAL POST Subscribe

NEWS · FULL COMMENT · SPORTS · CULTURE · LIFE · MORE · DRIVING · CLASSIFIEDS · JOBS · SUBSCRIBE · FINANCIAL POST

Professor at criminal justice school called students 'future dead cops.' He's been suspended

Michael Isaacson, an adjunct professor at CUNY's John Jay College of Criminal Justice, was placed on administrative leave because of a three-week-old tweet

By Kristine Phillips

Commissioner O'Neill @NYPDONeill

As a 2x grad there, I know Michael Isaacson's reprehensible values don't represent @JohnJayCollege, #NYC, #NYPD or families of murdered cops

8:52 PM - Sep 15, 2017

121 316 743

Bill de Blasio @NYCMayor

New York City won't stand for the vile anti-police rhetoric of Michael Isaacson and neither should John Jay College.

7:14 PM - Sep 15, 2017

393 198 593

And this is something that came up in the news recently about a professor who is teaching at a police college. He said that he had the honour of teaching "future dead cops." This did not go over well.

Canada

- Canadian Taxpayers Federation
    - Generation Screwed
- Mount Royal University
- Guelph University
    - Lou Reed's "Walk on the Wild Side"
- Wilfred Laurier University
    - Sandor Dosman, Veritas Café
    - Danielle Robitaille
- Ryerson University
    - Jane Mathias
        - My Name is Josephine YouTube page; Factual Feminist YouTube page (Christina Hoff Sommers)

Turning from England and the US to Canada, the suppression of free speech at home seems to be coming almost exclusively from the left side of the political spectrum. In terms of incidents that have happened, we have had the Canadian Taxpayers Federation promote their book *Generation Screwed*[22]. There have been university groups at the University of Laval and Guelph University that have prevented them from coming there. Some students are vocalizing that they don't like the Canadian Taxpayers Federation's brand of activism, while others are saying that they don't like the word "screwed" because it is offensive.

At Mount Royal University, the leader of the student union told a student to take off his Trump hat because wearing it made him racist. Someone can be a Trump supporter for a variety of reasons, but we often assume that that supporter agrees with everything that a candidate says when another option is that people may support a candidate despite their stance on key issues. In the absence of information or a discussion, how does the leader of a student union know whether a student's hat is being worn to promote racism?

This summer at Guelph University, a student group apologized for playing Lou Reed's song "Take a Walk on the Wild Side" because it is "transphobic." They then retracted their apology when they found out that Holly Woodlawn, the subject of the song, said that "Andy Warhol may have made me famous, but you [Lou Reed] have made me immortal." The student group clearly ended up looking foolish.

22 When I delivered my lecture, I did not know that *Generation Screwed* is also the title of a book written by Candice Malcolm, who runs *True North*.

At Wilfred Laurier University, Sandor Dosman, a café manager, published an ad because he was looking to hire a new employee. Because he was having trouble finding an employee, he used humour in which he relied on the hipster stereotype, stating that "we'll accept people with manbuns and tattoos and give low wages," but he was fired because he used the word "slave" in the ad. The student group that owned the café decided that the word "slave" was offensive and fired him.

Danielle Robitaille is a lawyer who attended Dalhousie University, where she won the Muriel Duckworth Award for "raising consciousness of women's issues and feminism in the legal community." She was supposed to give a talk about being a woman in the legal profession, but the university cancelled the talk because of "security concerns" since she was one of the lawyers who defended Jian Ghomeshi.

Ryerson University has been a hotbed for the suppression of free speech. The case of Jane Mathias went viral. In her sociology class, she wanted to write a paper on the wage gap. She emailed her professor about that and was told that she could use only feminist sources. In the course outline, there were more stipulations. The professor said students weren't allowed to use newspapers or data from the Government of Canada because they did not have the skills to interpret the numbers and data. She went on to say that the "patriarchy is real, so this is what you need to do."

Her sister, Josephine, then launched her "My Name is Josephine" YouTube page and argued that the wage gap is a myth. In those videos, Ms. Mathias quotes the feminist Christina Hoff Sommers. Interestingly, Sommers has a YouTube page called "The Factual Feminist," where she argues that the wage gap is a myth. The wage gap is an issue that seems to be catastrophic only because of the actions of university campuses; everywhere else, the gap is either much smaller than purported or even nonexistent.

FEATURES, FEMINISM, POLITICS

Published on July 15, 2017

Why It's Time To Stop Worrying About First World 'Gender Gaps'

written by **Aaron Neil**

Here is one example from July 2017 arguing that it's time to stop worrying about the issue since it's a problem only for first-world countries.

Canada

- Canadian Taxpayers Federation
  - Generation Screwed
- Mount Royal University
- Guelph University
  - Lou Reed's "Walk on the Wild Side"
- Wilfred Laurier University
  - Sandor Dosman, Veritas Café
  - Danielle Robitaille
- Ryerson University
  - Jane Mathias
    - My Name is Josephine YouTube page; Factual Feminist YouTube page
  - Men's Issues Awareness Society
  - Cancellation of Panel Discussion
    - The Stifling of Free Speech on University Campuses
    - Gad Saad, Concordia University, Marketing & Research Chair in Evolutionary Behavioural Sciences and Darwinian Consumption

Another issue of contention at Ryerson University involves a Men's Issues Awareness Society. What's interesting about this group is that there are more women than men in it. On other campuses, there is often a 50/50 mix of men and women in the men's rights group. Despite this, they were denied club status at Ryerson.

Most recently, there was a cancellation of a panel discussion that ironically was called "The Stifling of Free Speech on University Campuses." What's ironic about that, apart from the title, is that one of the people on the panel was Gad Saad, a professor of marketing and a researcher in evolutionary behavioural sciences and Darwinian consumption at Concordia University. He's a Jewish refugee from Lebanon who escaped religious persecution and is now being labeled a white supremacist just because he is arguing for the notion of free speech. I wonder what is happening here.[23]

23 Gad Saad and Jordan B. Peterson are among the few outspoken academics in Canada who have managed to keep their jobs as tenured professors. I hope that the reader will ask themselves what is so special about them that they get to keep their jobs when everyone else has either been silenced or has been excommunicated from academia. A fact that I find interesting is that Dr. Saad has served as an advisor for the Justice Centre for Constitutional Freedoms in the past (and may well be associated with them at the present) and that Dr. Peterson is the 2023 recipient of a "freedom award" from the Justice Centre for Constitutional Freedoms. Both of these academics have supplemented the income they have received from their universities with income that they have received from sources such as their Patreon accounts and the books that they sold after they attained fame. Given the amount of time that Drs. Saad and Peterson have invested in their political activities, I hope that the reader will agree that Drs. Saad and Peterson have used their positions as tenured professors to serve their personal interests instead of the public's interests, even though they were receiving income from taxpayer funded universities and are therefore expected to conduct themselves in ways that serve the interests of their students and the taxpayer.

THE GLOBE AND MAIL*

OPINION

We need to protect free speech on campus

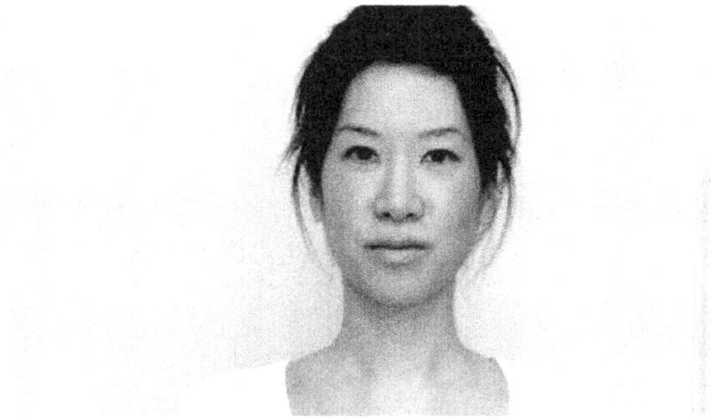

Debra Soh

DEBRA SOH
CONTRIBUTED TO THE GLOBE AND MAIL
JUNE 25, 2017

Debra Soh is a Toronto-based sex and political writer with a PhD in sexual neuroscience from York University.

This is an article that I found rather compelling. During the Harper era, there was much coverage about this administration silencing scientists, especially when it came to issues pertaining to the environment. At the time, we had groups such as the Canadian Association of University Teachers (CAUT) that were very active in countering the Harper government. It's interesting that these groups are now silent.[24] The only incident that they have commented on is the cancellation of the panel; they have been curiously silent about most issues of late, and one might wonder why that is.

I got some insight from Debra Soh.[25] She's a researcher in neuroscience. In this article, she explains that she decided to abandon academia because it's so stifling. Here she talks about what is happening behind the scenes:

> For example, in my field of sexology, even if academic researchers have tenure, they will avoid particular areas of study completely (such as the

24 The reason is more apparent now than it was when I delivered this lecture: Justin Trudeau's administration has long been pandering to CAUT and other activist groups.

25 Since I delivered this talk, Dr. Soh has published a book titled *The End of Gender: Debunking the Myths About Sex and Identity in Our Society.*

> topics of gender dysphoria in children or biological sex differences in the brain) because they know their professional and personal reputations will be at stake if their findings aren't socially palatable.
>
> It is also often the case that academics cannot interact with the media without explicit approval from their institution. As a result, the mainstream discourse suffers because only "experts" touting politically correct messages are heard. This results in a bias in information that is available to the public, and further indoctrination of a generation of students who are already shielded from dissenting views.

This is very similar to the Harper years, where you had the suppression of scientists who worked for the government, but this is now happening within the university setting.[26]

26 When I delivered this lecture, I did not understand that suppression of free speech was expected in return for the funding that Acadia University received from the federal and provincial governments to renovate their science building.

Debate on Bill C-16 at University of Toronto; November 19, 2016

Jordan B. Peterson, Department of Psychology, OPPOSED

Mayo Moran, Provost & Vice-Chancellor, MODERATOR

Brenda Cossman, Bonham Centre for Sexual Diversity Studies, FAVOUR

Mary Bryson; UBC; Institute for Gender, Race, Sexuality, and Social Justice; FAVOUR

One may wonder how someone can delve deeper into an issue if it's something they can't ask about. The best way to get an answer to this question is by asking what happens to people who speak out on that issue. The one who is most famous for this would be Jordan B. Peterson. I will approach his case by examining the mechanics of how he has been treated instead of the substance of his stance on Bill C-16. Interestingly, it appears that the only place where his trials and tribulations have been reported has been in the *National Post,* with very little in the more liberal media.

I'll now ask you [the audience] if the following structure sounds reasonable for a debate: We have a moderator, one person who is in favour of a position, and one person who is opposed. We let them both speak, and the moderator makes sure that there's equal time for both sides of the issue. Afterwards, the moderator opens up the floor to questions from the audience. Does that sound like a reasonable approach? [The audience agreed.]

Now we will look at what actually happened in the debate on Bill C-16 that took place at the University of Toronto on November 19, 2016. The gist of Bill C-16 is that the government was going to add gender identity and gender expression to the Human Rights and Criminal Code. Peterson was opposed to that.

Peterson went against two people instead of just one person.

Before I forget, I want to give you a heads up now that the suppression of free speech is often done under the guise of social justice, and the terms that will keep coming up over and over again in the rest of this talk will be equity, diversity, and inclusion—these seem to be the buzz words.

Turning back to the debate, we have Jordan Peterson going up against Brenda Cossman and Mary Bryson, i.e., two people instead of one. In their opening remarks, Brenda Cossman commends all the people who are banning this event, and Mary Bryson says that these issues are not up for debate. Earlier in this talk, I argued that it was unacceptable when the Harper government claimed that issues were not up for debate; if it was unacceptable for the Harper government to assert that issues are not up for debate, then I would argue that it's also unacceptable for Mary Bryson to assert that an issue is not up for debate.

Let's now consider the actions of the moderator, Mayo Moran. Instead of allowing the debate to go back and forth, Moran allowed Jordan Peterson to argue his position and then allowed Brenda or Mary to do a rebuttal, but she did not allow Peterson to respond to the rebuttal. This was the format for this entire "debate."

For the question and answer period, the audience's questions were vetted by a committee who decided which questions would be asked. In other words, the audience didn't have a chance to ask any questions. One might begin to get a bit suspicious about what is happening behind the scenes.[27]

Fast forward to January 2017, when the Runnymede Society at Queen's University wanted to hold a debate on Bill C-16, they approached six professors in their faculty of law and not one of them wanted to debate Jordan Peterson. In the end Bruce Pardy, who agrees with Peterson, said he would play devil's advocate.[28] If you like, you can watch that debate, which is posted on YouTube.

27 A question that I did not think to ask at the time is: Why did Jordan Peterson agree to participate in a debate with the format that was used? It made sense for Cossman and Bryson to agree to this format because they knew that their views couldn't withstand scrutiny. But in the case of Peterson, I strongly suspect that he agreed to this format because he knew that such a biased format would work in his favour when it came to public relations.

28 An interesting fact about Bruce Pardy is that he has been on the Board of the Justice Centre for Constitutional Freedoms. What is the likelihood that all three of the outspoken Canadian academics who I have referenced in this talk would, by chance alone, have connections with the Justice Centre for Constitutional Freedoms?

Jordan B. Peterson: McMaster University (March 19, 2017)

- McMaster University Presidential Advisory Committee on Building an Inclusive Community (PACBIC)
- Patrick Deane (President, McMaster University)

On March 19, 2017, at McMaster University, there was supposed to be a panel discussion on free speech and political correctness in academic settings. There were supposed to be three panelists: two dropped out due to emails that they received and one because of security concerns. It ended up being just Jordan Peterson in a room like this, with all these protestors yelling obscenities at him such as "Transphobic piece of...," and the event was cancelled. The McMaster University Presidential Advisory Council Committee on Building an Inclusive Community was in favour of this cancellation. They concluded that there is no role for biology in this discussion and that the issue is solved. This announcement was followed by Patrick Deane's message stating that this was just a peaceful protest.

thestar.com

Your Toronto · Schools

University of Toronto gets ready for first-ever Black graduation ceremony

Event planned by students for grads from all programs on three campuses follows in footsteps of Harvard and other U.S. schools.

Another disturbing trend is racial segregation. The University of Toronto readily supported a request that came from a student group for a black graduation ceremony. The University of Toronto contributed funding to this event, and Kelly Hannah-Moffatt, the Vice President of Human Resources and Equity, was very enthusiastic about it.

In case I didn't communicate this point earlier in this lecture, a lot of words that are used may sound rather benign but have a darker meaning when one compares how these words are typically used (or are properly understood) to the new way in which they are now being used.[29]

29 At the time, I did not realize that I was referencing George Orwell's *1984*.

Acadia University

- Doxing by alt right

Turning from what is happening at other universities to what is happening in our own backyard, I note that there was a doxing incident that occurred over the summer that was done by an alt-right group. Doxing refers to the sharing of personal information about people without their permission. I looked at the Twitter feed of the group that had done this and traced the doxing incident to a protest that happened in Halifax on Canada Day concerning the Cornwallis statues. The media blew this incident out of proportion and treated it as if it were one characterized by violence.

Sign In/Register Subscribe

NATIONAL POST

NEWS FULL COMMENT SPORTS CULTURE LIFE MORE DRIVING CLASSIFIEDS JOBS SUBSCRIBE FINANCIAL POST

Christie Blatchford: Proud Boys' behaviour might be goofy, but is hardly 'deplorable'

Not a blow was struck. Not a disrespectful word uttered. Then the men were outed as Canadian Forces members and soon were tossed under the bus by their leaders

Members of Proud Boys Maritimes at an encounter with protesters in Halifax.

CBC radio

Day 6

with Brent Bambury

EPISODES FEATURES ABOUT CONTACT

Friday July 21, 2017

Indigenous children are dying while Ottawa fights a ruling that calls for action

The journalist Christie Blatchford[30] analyzed the video footage from that day and concluded that some people may have been foolish in their conduct, but that nothing happened beyond that. If you watch the video, you can decide for yourself. In terms of what happened, there was a conversation between the members of the Proud Boys and some native activists. Afterward, Antifa doxed the Proud Boys, which led to them being disciplined by the military. Then this alt-right group that is based in Cape Breton become angry about the incident and decided to dox multiple people, including members of our community which included LGBTQ activists, some students, and a faculty member.[31] One characteristic that they have in common is that they self-identify as feminists. My fear in the summer was that the situation would escalate, but it appears that nothing happened after this incident.

While the activists have directed their anger at statues and have received much media attention for doing so, we tend to lose focus on the more pressing issues, such as many First Nations communities not having drinking water even though the Trudeau government has been in power for two years. We also have people such as Cindy Blackstock,[32] who has been arguing for child services in northern Ontario but to no avail. In fact, our courts have informed the government that it is time to act. This is where we should be focusing our attention instead of on the statues.

30 This journalist went on to become a recipient of a "freedom award" from the Justice Centre for Constitutional Freedoms in 2019.

31 The faculty member turned out to be Erin Crandall (Department of Politics), who was a participant on the panel discussion on free speech that I had hosted in May 2017 and who was in attendance at my talk.

32 I find it interesting that Cindy Blackstock would later go on to submit a formal complaint against me because she disagreed with some of my posts on social media.

Acadia University

- Doxing by alt right
- Students, faculty, and staff feel uncomfortable expressing their views
  - "You can't say THAT in a university"
- Uncritical acceptance of social justice, but little appreciation of other views
- Campus during Harper versus Trudeau eras
  - Debt
  - Proportional representation
  - Phoenix payroll system
  - Minimal protests over CETA (Comprehensive Economic and Trade Agreement)

At Acadia University, a number of students have told me that they feel uncomfortable voicing their opinions in their classes or expressing their views on campus because they fear being ostracized. One way to find out if this is more than just my impression is by administering a tool called the Fearless Speech Index so that we can analyze objective data on this issue. In the meantime, I will continue to report my observations.

When I sent an open letter to the Acadia community in August, there was silence on the email server, but I received many phone calls and email messages from students and staff thanking me for the message I had sent. In large part, they kept saying, "I'm afraid to speak out for myself." Interestingly, when I emailed the campus the details of the talk that I am delivering today, all the ones who were supportive of me messaged me privately, whereas the people who claim that I am oppressing them expressed their views in public forums. Other people have told me that there are topics that can be discussed only outside of the university bubble.

I have also observed an uncritical approval of anything related to social justice and a lack of political diversity on campus. For example, you can easily find posters for talks by the Canadian Council on Policy Alternatives, but you don't hear much about talks by groups such as the Canadian Taxpayers Federation or the Frasier Institute. Similarly, if someone wanted to hear a talk by a member of the trans community, the only options available at university campuses are viewpoints from the left; for example, one should not expect to hear from people like Theryn Meyer or Blair White at this campus.

As well, I have noticed university professors parroting slogans such as "Because it's 2015."[33] For example, I heard this slogan at a convocation for

33 When I delivered my talk, I did not know that Prime Minister Trudeau was making reference to the UN's Agenda 2030, or what we now know as "The Great Reset."

science and noticed that a professor of biology has included it in the signature of the email messages that she sends.[34] I find the obsession with this slogan morbidly fascinating because one cannot use the current year as a logical argument for anything. For example, try using "because it's 2017" to get out of a parking ticket; it's not going to work.[35]

On a related note, I have seen numerous emails that have made reference to the slogan "diversity is our strength," which I find meaningless. Instead of "diversity" being a strength, I would argue that being able to reach a consensus even though we all have differences of opinion would be an example of a strength.

Last year, I remember Justin Trudeau talking at the UN about how he was a feminist; this talk spread like wildfire on campus. I found that interesting, given his record of selling arms to Saudi Arabia. It's not as if this country has the best record when it comes to women's rights. To the contrary, it's only today that women in Saudi Arabia have the right to drive.

It's been rather interesting comparing the campus throughout the Harper years with the Trudeau years. Harper couldn't do the slightest thing without having some criticism, but now, during the Trudeau years, there is suddenly a silence.

My argument is that Trudeau's record is quite abysmal.[36] We can look at his long list of broken promises, including what our debt would look like and proportional representation. There's also the issue of the Phoenix payroll system, which has resulted in a lot of government employees who haven't been paid; two years is a bit overkill for the Trudeau administration to now say that this is Stephen Harper's fault. As well, I'm surprised that there's been little to no protest over CETA (Comprehensive Economic and Trade Agreement), which has gone through with minimal protest. I'm not sure if you know this, but your prices for prescription drugs are about to go up in seven years.

When it comes to political power, the shelf life for a party in Canada is either eight or twelve years (2 or 3 terms of 4 years per term; it is rare for an incumbent party to not get re-elected to a second term in Canada). This means that the Trudeau administration is counting on someone else to take the blame for his administration's actions.

34 I did not mention this point during my talk, but the person I was referring to was Glenys Gibson. Dr. Gibson is a feminist and is now Head of the Department of Biology at Acadia University.

35 Interestingly, my last research presentation as a tenured professor was titled "The Relationship Between Political Orientation and Bullshit Detection: A Pilot Study." In this study, my student and I found that roughly 50% of self-described liberals/progressives classified "Because it's 2017" as bullshit, whereas 66% to 88% of people with other political orientations classified this statement as bullshit.

36 After my talk, a number of students who were majoring in politics informed me that they heard more criticisms of Justin Trudeau in my talk than they had in all of the politics courses that they had taken since Justin Trudeau was sworn in as Prime Minister in November 2015.

NATIONAL POST

NEWS · FULL COMMENT · SPORTS · CULTURE · LIFE · MORE · DRIVING · CLASSIFIEDS · JOBS · SUBSCRIBE · FINANCIAL POST

Kelly McParland: The Liberals over-promise and under-deliver on the Indigenous file

The inquiry into missing and murdered Indigenous women reflects how ineffective both Ottawa and Indigenous groups are at finding workable solutions

TV RADIO NEWS SPORTS MUSIC LIFE ARTS CANADA 2017 LOCAL ▾ MORE ▾ WATCH LISTEN LOG I

CBCnews | Opinion

Home | Opinion | World | Canada | Politics | Business | Health | Entertainment | Technology & Science | Video

Home

OPINION | A truly feminist government would consider the plight of Indigenous men: Robyn Urback

The Liberals are being asked to widen the scope of the MMIW inquiry to include missing and murdered men

By Robyn Urback, CBC News Posted: Dec 09, 2016 5:00 AM ET | Last Updated: Dec 09, 2016 5:00 AM ET

A coalition called Expand the Inquiry is asking the federal government to broaden the scope of its national inquiry into missing and murdered Indigenous women to include Indigenous men. (CBC)

As one example of why I am worried about the future of our country, the Liberals made big promises regarding the murdered and missing indigenous women but have made little progress on that file. On one hand, there's going to be anger amongst the indigenous community, but outside of that community, there will also be anger from people questioning why we are spending this money when we have nothing to show for it. With multiple groups angry for different reasons, we have the roots of social unrest planted.

Within the indigenous community, there have been groups advocating for an expanded inquiry for men. One of their arguments is that more men have been affected than women. But the answer has been a consistent "no."

cbcnews | Opinion

Home Opinion World Canada Politics Business Health Entertainment Technology & Science Video

Home

OPINION | The budget's gender-based analysis forgot to look at one thing — men: Neil Macdonald

Men are falling behind in education and losing their jobs in the resource and manufacturing sectors

By Neil Macdonald, CBC News Posted: Mar 28, 2017 5:00 AM ET | Last Updated: Mar 28, 2017 5:00 AM ET

There are a few things the budget's gender-based analysis ignores, and might be worth addressing next time. (Sean Kilpatrick/Canadian Press)

Global NEWS Halifax Change Location TV News Programs Newscasts & Videos

World Canada Local Politics Smart Living Money Entertainment Health Commentary Trending Sports Video More Follow Like

September 17, 2017 Updated: September 17, 2017

Trudeau government looks to limit debate on big priorities as Parliament returns

By Joanna Smith The Canadian Press

Comments Facebook 1.8k Twitter Email Print ...

WATCH ABOVE: Tale of two caucuses: Liberals and Conservatives prepare for fall session

Related to the issue of gender relations, we recently had a budget with a preamble about how it differentially affects men and women. After that, the focus of the budget is exclusively on women. If men express concern about being excluded from the political system, they are told that "we are not going to have that debate."

B **Views among college students regarding the First Amendment: Results from a new survey**

Controversial speakers

One way to examine tolerance to offensive speech is to explore views on what actions students deem permissible to prevent it from occurring. The next two questions are based on the following scenario:

A public university invites a very controversial speaker to an on-campus event. The speaker is known for making offensive and hurtful statements.

The survey included a set of questions considering student views regarding actions aimed at disrupting the speech:

A student group opposed to the speaker disrupts the speech by loudly and repeatedly shouting so that the audience cannot hear the speaker. Do you agree or disagree that the student group's actions are acceptable?

		Political Affiliation			Type of College		Gender	
	All	Dem	Rep	Ind	Public	Private	Female	Male
Agree	51	62	39	45	51	51	47	57
Disagree	49	38	61	55	49	49	53	43

On a related note, evidence for another disturbing trend comes from the results of a survey that was administered in the US. In this survey, 40–60% of respondents from across the political spectrum agreed that it is acceptable to shout down speakers.

B Views among college students regarding the First Amendment: Results from a new survey

A student group opposed to the speaker uses violence to prevent the speaker from speaking. Do you agree or disagree that the student group's actions are acceptable?

		Political Affiliation			Type of College		Gender	
	All	**Dem**	**Rep**	**Ind**	**Public**	**Private**	**Female**	**Male**
Agree	19	20	22	16	18	21	10	30
Disagree	81	80	78	84	82	79	90	70

Furthermore, this survey asked whether it is acceptable to use violence if you disagree with the speaker. Roughly 20% said yes. This is a very disturbing finding, especially when you consider that these people are going to be your future lawmakers. This survey was taken last week.

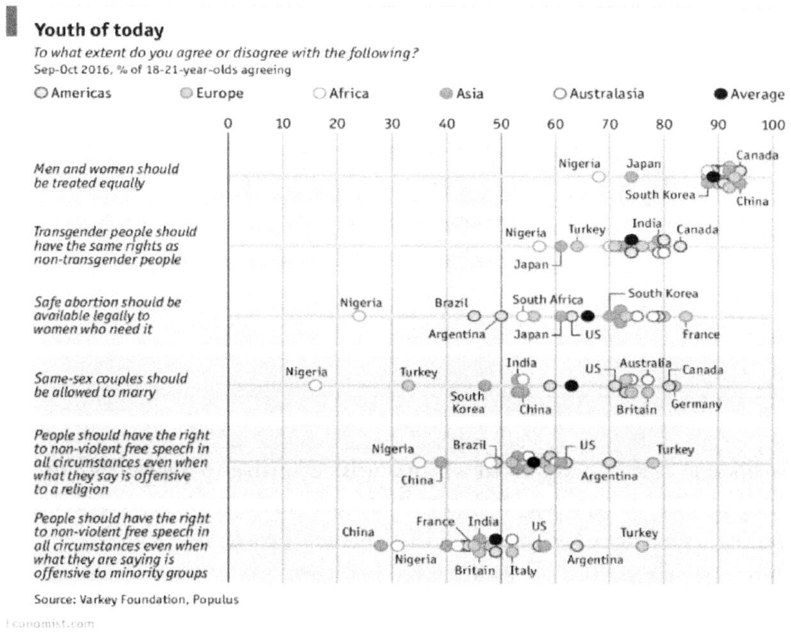

And this is from a fairly large-scale survey done across numerous countries in which young people were asked about their views on different issues. Generally, we observe that people are supportive of gender equality, transgender rights, abortion, and even same-sex marriage. So there is really high approval there, but what they do disapprove of is anything that would offend people who are religious or visible minorities. I see that as a dangerous trend as someone who is a visible minority because that gives me protected status that others don't have. That is called "weaponized victimhood" or "victimhood weaponization," where I can use my skin colour against someone else with relative impunity.

INDEPENDENT News InFact Politics Voices Indy/Life Business Sport Tech Culture Subscribe

News › World › Americas

White professor was fired from predominantly black university due to colour of skin, court rules

The $5m awarded to Beverly Wilkins by a jury will also remain in place

Mythili Sampathkumar New York @MythiliSk Tuesday 13 June 2017 16:31 BST 10 comments

Here is a recent example of racism directed at a white professor. Professor Beverly Wilkins started her position in 2001. In 2007, a professor by the name of Leticia Smith started, and over the course of three years she got promoted to assistant dean and then dean. In 2010, Smith dismissed Wilkins under the pretext of budgetary cuts. Smith ended up hiring someone who earned $15,000 more than Wilkins. When there was a further investigation, they found out that everyone who was let go was white except for one person. This is why there was a 5-million-dollar lawsuit over discrimination. The point here is that no one should have a special status based on their ethnicity or religion.

Contributing Factors: Strands of an Intricate Web

- Modern social climate
  - How we get our news and communicate

Now that I have characterized the problem, the next step for me is to identify the contributing factors.[37]

There have been large changes in my lifetime in terms of how we communicate. Before, we used to have print media with different sources and were able to debate different points of view. These days, we get our information from the internet, where the information is often filtered for us, and we can decide what we want to get for ourselves. We can also minimize our interactions with people with whom we disagree, and that changes the kinds of information to which we are exposed and how we communicate that information.

37 I used the words "Strand of an Intricate Web" to describe the contributing factors to the problems of our time in this presentation. In my video titled "Silencing Dissent" (which I posted on October 30, 2019), I used the words "Components of a Perfect Storm." Nowadays, I would use the words "Web of Deceit" to describe the conditions under which we live. One nice characteristic about this web is that it has become so large and unwieldy that it is getting ready to fold on itself.

Social Media "Filter Bubbles" as a Medium for Group Polarization

Like-minds network in the blogosphere. Blue liberal blogs link mostly to one another, as do red conservative blogs, with each blog's size reflecting the number of other blogs linking to it (From Lazer et al., 2009.) ww.ncbi.nlm.nih.gov/pmc/articles/PMC2745217/]

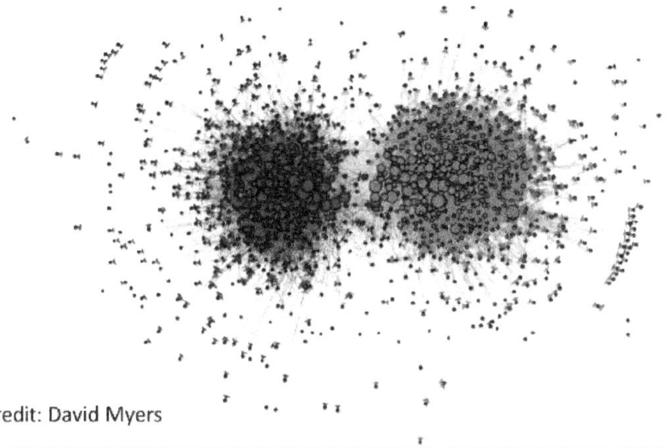

Slide credit: David Myers

This picture shows what is happening quite nicely. In this picture are the blogospheres in the United States of people who are Republicans and Democrats. This picture shows how the two groups of people are living in their own little worlds and are separate from one another.

Contributing Factors: Strands of an Intricate Web

- Modern social climate
  - How we get our news and communicate
  - Opposing views are perceived as threats to identity → discrimination
    - We have always had ways of separating ourselves into us vs them
      - Us – having positive qualities and being diverse
      - Them – having negative qualities and all being similar
    - Question of debate
      - Has tolerance for diversity in backgrounds led to an intolerance for opposing viewpoints?

Another trend that worries me is that human beings have always had a tendency to separate the world into "us" and "them." In the past, this has been on the basis of race, gender, or sexual orientation; these are ways that we can separate ourselves into "us" versus "them," with "us" being morally superior, having good qualities, and being different from one another, and with "them" being inferior and all being the same.

A question that comes to mind is whether we are using viewpoints in a similar fashion. A recent study by Bizumic et al. (2017) suggests that is what is happening.

Bizumic et al. (2017)

- Scale of Ethnic Tolerance
  - High agreement with statements such as...
    - "The values, ways of life, and customs of other cultures are probably just as good as my own"
    - "I like the idea of a society in which people from completely different cultures, ethnic groups, and backgrounds mix together freely"
  - Low agreement with a statement such as...
    - "The world would be a much better place if all other cultures and ethnic groups modelled themselves on my culture"

In this study, which was published earlier this year, the researchers (Bizumic et al., 2017) administered a scale of ethnic tolerance in multiple studies. This scale consisted of different statements, and participants were asked to rate how much they agreed with the various statements using a scale of 1 to 9. You would be highly tolerant if you agreed with statements such as "The values, ways of life, and customs of other cultures are probably just as good as my own" and if you disagreed with statements like this one: "The world would be a much better place if all other cultures and ethnic groups modelled themselves on my culture." In other words, high scores on the first statement and low scores on the latter statement are expected from a person who has a high ethnic tolerance score.

A strength of the studies in this report is that the samples are more representative of the population than in many other studies in psychology because the authors administered their surveys to community groups as opposed to student groups.

Bizumic et al. (2017)

- Study 1b
  - Done in Australia with a sample consisting of students and community (n = 188, mean age = 30.21 years, 61.17% female), paper & pencil
  - All participants completed measure of Ethnic Tolerance
  - Then presented with a statement advocating for or against mandatory detention of asylum seekers
    - Asked to rate how much they accepted/rejected the statement and whether they would accept/reject having the person who made the statement in their lives
  - Findings
    - High on Ethnic Tolerance – more likely to reject "for" statement than "against" statement, reject the person for both intimate and non-intimate relationships
    - Low on Ethic Tolerance – more likely to reject "against" statement than "for" statement, but did not discriminate on either measure of social distance

In Bizumic et al.'s first study, the researchers administered their materials using a paper and pencil test. Everyone was given a scale of ethnic tolerance and was then given a statement either advocating for or against the mandatory detention of asylum seekers. In addition to rating the statements, the participants were asked whether they would accept or reject the person who made the statements—in the sense of being a friend or a neighbour versus an intimate relationship like a lover. The researchers found that the people who scored high on the scale of ethnic tolerance were more likely to reject the people who were in favour of mandatory detention for both intimate and non-intimate relationships. In other words, they (the people who score high on ethnic tolerance) rejected not only the argument with which they disagreed but also the person who made the argument in any capacity.

This pattern was not observed in those who scored low on ethnic tolerance. In other words, they were likely to oppose mandatory detention of asylum seekers, but this was independent of their rejection or acceptance of another person as a human being.

Bizumic et al. (2017)

- Study 2
  - High on Ethnical Tolerant showed political intolerance towards those in favour of mandatory detention
      - Agreeing with "they should be banned from running for public office"
    - Also showed more prejudice
  - Low on Ethnic Tolerance did not show political intolerance or prejudice towards those against mandatory detention
- Study 3
  - Similar results found in the US in the context of prejudice
  - Online study (Qualtrics)
  - Controlled for political ideology
- Study 4
  - Conducted in UK
  - Assess whether the prejudice is due to moral convictions and/or identity

We see the same kind of findings in the second study done by the authors. This study asked about ethnic tolerance in the context of political intolerance. Instead of asking whether the participants would be friends with or have an intimate relationship with a person who had a specific point of view, the participants were asked if they would vote for someone who had these views. In this study, the researchers found that participants who scored high on ethnic tolerance agreed with statements stating that those who disagreed should be banned from public office. These participants also scored highly on a measure of prejudice against those people. That's something we did not see in the group that scored low on the ethnic tolerance scale.

In the third study, which was an online study, the researchers replicated the main findings and corrected for political ideology. The idea is that similar results were found after statistically controlling for people's positions on the political spectrum.

In the fourth study, the researchers attempted to figure out whether their results could be explained by a measure of moral convictions or how people identify with one another.

Bizumic et al. (2017), Study 4

Ethnic tolerance and out-group intolerance B. Bizumic *et al.*

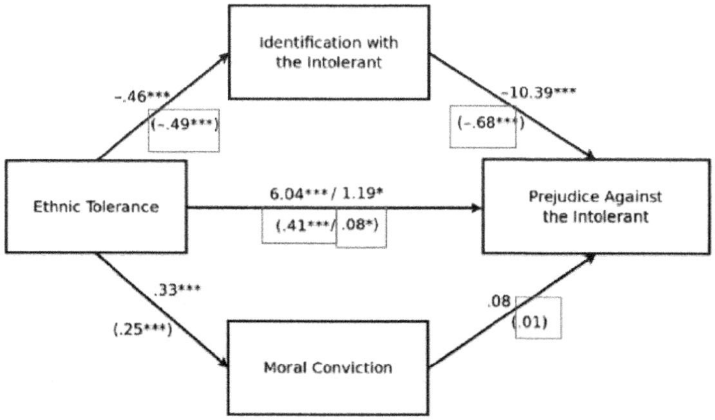

Fig. 3: A mediation analysis representing effects of ethnic tolerance on prejudice against the intolerant through identification and moral conviction. Liberalism was a covariate in models predicting the mediating variables and the dependent variable. Both non-standardized and standardized (in parentheses) coefficients are presented. *Note*: $^*p < .05$, $^{***}p < .001$

As a starting point for this slide, I will state that the variable of interest is the relationship between "ethnic tolerance" and "prejudice against the intolerant." The strength of this relationship varies between 0 and 1; thus, the larger the number, the stronger the relationship. Apart from having a value between 0 and 1, the relationship can be either positive or negative. In terms of the relationship between ethnic tolerance and prejudice, the slide shows that the strength of this relationship is .41 if the other variables in their study are not taken into consideration and that the strength of this relationship decreases to .08 when the researchers include "moral conviction" and their measure of "identification with the intolerant" in their analysis.

If we look at the moral conviction side of the slide (the bottom half of the above figure), there does seem to be a relationship between ethnic tolerance and moral conviction, but there is no relationship between ethic tolerance and prejudice against the intolerant once moral conviction is taken into consideration. The researchers thus concluded that the rejection of the intolerant had nothing to do with moral convictions.

Let's now turn to the identification side. This part of the figure shows that the more ethnic tolerance you have, the less likely you are to identify with someone that you view as intolerant. The strength of that connection is about -.5, so it is moderately strong. The less you identify with that person, the more likely you are to exhibit prejudice against this person who has a different point of view; the strength of this connection is almost -.7.

Essentially, if we see someone with a different point of view, we see them as an outlier and we're more likely to dislike them on that basis.

Interestingly, the data for these studies were collected between 2010 and 2014, and were published in 2017. In other words, the data were collected well before things became even more "heated" on the world stage.

I suspect that these relationships would be even stronger if the study were replicated in the current political climate, especially if the researchers collected data from a sample of the activist community, where the views are more polarized.

The key point that I want to make is that the intolerance observed by those who scored high on ethic tolerance was observed before Donald Trump became president; this is contrary to the argument that Donald Trump's presidency caused the United States to become a polarized nation.[38]

38 In this section of my talk, I was referring to the strong reaction in the media to Donald Trump's presidency, e.g., the references in the media to us living in a "post-truth world."

Contributing Factors: Strands of an Intricate Web

- Modern social climate
  - How we get our news and communicate
  - Opposing views are perceived as threats to identity
  - Approaches to activism

There are a variety of ways that one can act when they are living in a polarized world. My actions today are inspired by a person who I idolized when I was a child: the Indian activist Mohandas K. Gandhi (Mahatma Gandhi).[39] His goal was to show his oppressors the error of their ways.

During my childhood, I was often isolated, in part because I was one of the only brown children in my elementary school. I was also overweight and lacked both social skills and athletic ability. This made socializing with my peers difficult. An additional complication is that I had little in my childhood when it came to role models that I could look up to.

At the age of 10, I discovered Mohandas K. Gandhi when I watched the movie "Gandhi." What inspired me about him was that, under British rule, he didn't want to approach his enemies the way that a Marxist would. The idea was that he criticized evil deeds instead of saying that the British are evil people. His goal was to separate the person from their actions and to show his oppressors the error of their ways so that they would appreciate that what they were doing was wrong. He ultimately wanted them to realize that what they were doing was wrong and to leave on their own accord and as friends. He aspired to live in a country where everyone would be able to get along with each other despite their differences.[40]

When it came to his views on spirituality, he would say that "we might have different paths, but our destination is the same."[41] He tried to look at the inherent goodness in people and aspired to bring out the best in them.

39 My first book, *A Service for the People*, makes clear that my later actions would be inspired by a variety of my favourite movie characters, which include Batman, Spider-Man, Harry Callahan, Sherlock Holmes, Tom Cruise's character in *A Few Good Men*, Bruce Lee's character in *Enter the Dragon*, and various characters from Monty Python's *Life of Brian*.

40 During my childhood, I did not understand that Mahatma Gandhi was fallible because he was only a human being. I eventually came to realize that I would be disappointed if I relied on a human being to be a perfect role model. That's because there is only one perfect role model for humanity: Jesus Christ.

41 I have come to learn that this statement is false, especially if one were to include Satanism as one of the world's religions as part of a discussion or debate.

In contrast, when I observe activists these days, I always find it disheartening to see them with their signs screaming at people. What I also see with modern activism are people who are self-appointed representatives of their communities and who impose their will by screaming at people. People, of course, are fearful of them and give in to their demands, as demonstrated by their silence.[42]

42 I did not realize this fact when I delivered my talk, but I was describing the adult version of bullying.

The Harvard Crimson SEARCH

NEWS OPINION FEATURES MAGAZINE SPORTS ARTS FLYBY

I'm a Female Minority at Harvard, and I Don't Agree with PC Culture

BY NATALIE BAO TRAM LE June 13, 2017

TV RADIO NEWS SPORTS MUSIC LIFE ARTS CANADA 2017 LOCAL MORE WATCH LISTEN LOG IN

CBCnews | Opinion

Home Opinion World Canada Politics Business Health Entertainment Technology & Science Video

Home

OPINION | I'm black and gay. Black Lives Matter Toronto doesn't speak for me

I believe Toronto police should be allowed to participate in Pride in their uniforms

By Orville Lloyd Douglas, for CBC News Posted: Jun 12, 2017 5:00 AM ET | Last Updated: Jun 12, 2017 5:00 AM ET

I can honestly say I feel uncomfortable at Caribana due to black homophobia, which Black Lives Matter casually ignores. (Mark Blinch/The Canadian Press)

However, every once in a while, you'll hear from someone. And when they speak, it's actually quite interesting to hear what they have to say.

Here is a letter written by a Harvard student named Natalie Bao Tram Le, who submitted the following to the Harvard Crimson:

> I share the same LGBT demographic with the protesters that stood and held up "Fight Transphobia" signs, but they do not speak for me—especially as they infringe upon free speech and expression. Being part of a protected class does not give us the privilege or right to shut down speech just because we do not like what we hear. As a demographic whose cause is founded on tolerance and acceptance, we are hypocritical for supporting PC culture.
>
> What the protesters are actually doing is selfish. They are pushing their own agenda in hopes of preventing people, including a female

> minority like me, from being exposed to differing opinions that challenge them to think critically. Furthermore, the fact that they—and many other college protesters—equate speech with violence is concerning, since this logic can easily be used to excuse tactics that encroach on people's free speech.

We see the same kind of thing in this article that was published in the CBC about Black Lives Matter. At the Black Lives Matter protest that the author is referencing, the police ended up not wearing their uniforms. Orville Lloyd Douglas denounces that action in this article. He argues that the police have apologized for past transgressions and that they're making headway in the gay community by making amends for the past. Meanwhile, there were events in Toronto like Caribana, which is an event for the black community, in which there's open homophobia but in which Black Lives Matter does absolutely nothing. Douglas concludes this article by stating that Black Lives Matter does not speak for him.

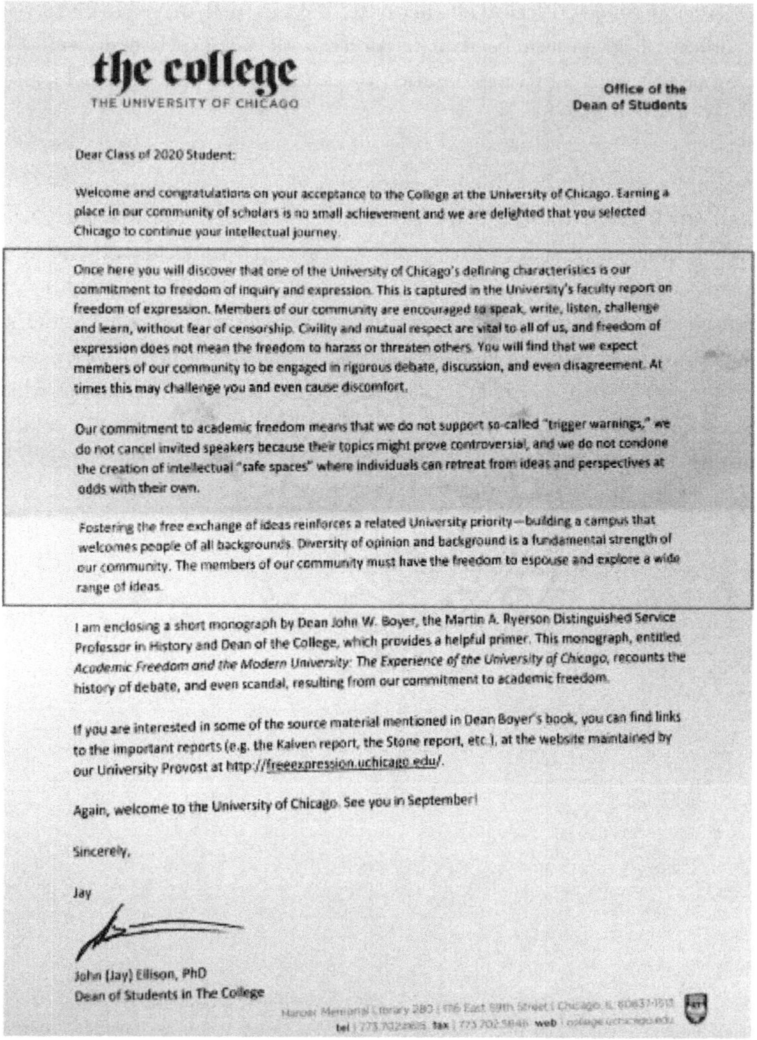

the college
THE UNIVERSITY OF CHICAGO

Office of the
Dean of Students

Dear Class of 2020 Student:

Welcome and congratulations on your acceptance to the College at the University of Chicago. Earning a place in our community of scholars is no small achievement and we are delighted that you selected Chicago to continue your intellectual journey.

Once here you will discover that one of the University of Chicago's defining characteristics is our commitment to freedom of inquiry and expression. This is captured in the University's faculty report on freedom of expression. Members of our community are encouraged to speak, write, listen, challenge and learn, without fear of censorship. Civility and mutual respect are vital to all of us, and freedom of expression does not mean the freedom to harass or threaten others. You will find that we expect members of our community to be engaged in rigorous debate, discussion, and even disagreement. At times this may challenge you and even cause discomfort.

Our commitment to academic freedom means that we do not support so-called "trigger warnings," we do not cancel invited speakers because their topics might prove controversial, and we do not condone the creation of intellectual "safe spaces" where individuals can retreat from ideas and perspectives at odds with their own.

Fostering the free exchange of ideas reinforces a related University priority—building a campus that welcomes people of all backgrounds. Diversity of opinion and background is a fundamental strength of our community. The members of our community must have the freedom to espouse and explore a wide range of ideas.

I am enclosing a short monograph by Dean John W. Boyer, the Martin A. Ryerson Distinguished Service Professor in History and Dean of the College, which provides a helpful primer. This monograph, entitled *Academic Freedom and the Modern University: The Experience of the University of Chicago*, recounts the history of debate, and even scandal, resulting from our commitment to academic freedom.

If you are interested in some of the source material mentioned in Dean Boyer's book, you can find links to the important reports (e.g. the Kalven report, the Stone report, etc.), at the website maintained by our University Provost at http://freeexpression.uchicago.edu/.

Again, welcome to the University of Chicago. See you in September!

Sincerely,

Jay

John (Jay) Ellison, PhD
Dean of Students in The College

I have long wondered: Where do activists get the idea that the way to have their concerns addressed is by making demands of others and telling others that their way is the right way, as if the activists are arbiters of truth? That is, they won't even consider another person's point of view or the possibility that they may be mistaken in their beliefs or their understanding of the facts. They won't even try to win people over to their point of view by using persuasive arguments.

The answer to my question is: Marxist educators, especially if they happen to be unionized. I will now explain how I know this to be true.

Last year at this time, the University of Chicago issued a letter to all students about academic freedom (see above). The first boxed paragraph states that "this [commitment to freedom of inquiry and expression] is captured in the university faculty's report on freedom of expression." This sentence implies that a process in which all voices were allowed to participate had been completed and that the letter that Dean Ellson was writing was based on the end result of a democratic process.

Dean Ellson goes to state that:

> Members of our community are encouraged to speak, write, listen, challenge and learn, without fear of censorship. Civility and mutual respect are vital to all of us and freedom of expression does not mean freedom to harass or threaten others. You will find that we expect members of our community to be engaged in rigorous debate, discussion, and even disagreement. At times this may challenge you and even cause discomfort.

I think this is in line with what I try to do in class by having respectful discussions where we hope to convince someone that a point is true but can at the very least agree to disagree if someone is not convinced that a point is true.

The second paragraph is about trigger warnings. The issue with trigger warnings is that some universities are mandating them. At the University of Chicago, the administration's position is that they will not mandate trigger warnings but that professors can use them if they wish. Thus, professors can exercise their discretion when it comes to the issue of whether trigger warnings are warranted.

Regarding the issue of safe spaces, some universities have a puppy room or a room in which students can play with play-doh and crayons if they feel uncomfortable because of controversial speakers. The University of Chicago was saying that they would not have safe spaces like that just because people disagreed with a speaker. While some might argue that Dean Ellson's wording comes across as condescending, the dean was stating a fact.

The last part of his letter states:

> Fostering the free exchange of ideas reinforces a related University priority—building a campus that welcomes people of all backgrounds. Diversity of opinion and background is a fundamental strength of our community. The members of our community must have the freedom to espouse and explore a wide range of ideas.

One would be hard-pressed to find anything unreasonable in this letter.

The Chicago Maroon

Letter: Faculty Respond To Ellison With A Letter Of Their Own

"Contention [in discourse] has to be based on a commitment to learning from a wealth of histories and experiences—to more discussion, not less; to openness, not closure."

By Letter to the Editor

Dear Students of the Class of 2020:

As you have undoubtedly noticed, you and your new institution have been in the media spotlight lately. We want to take this opportunity to voice our own welcome as members of the faculty. You will find the University of Chicago to be a diverse place full of strong-minded people. We encourage you to become one of them.

Those of us who have signed this letter have a variety of opinions about requests for trigger warnings and safe spaces. We may also disagree as to whether free speech is ever legitimately interrupted by concrete pressures of the political. That is as it should be. But let there be no mistake: such requests often touch on substantive, ongoing issues of bias, intolerance, and trauma that affect our intellectual exchanges. To start a conversation by declaring that such requests are not worth making is an affront to the basic principles of liberal education and participatory democracy.

Foremost, we are committed to our students and to the free exchange of ideas. As teachers, we understand ourselves to be engaged in a collaborative experiment in the classroom. For that to work, mutual respect is indeed indispensable—all the more so since the practice of academic freedom can sometimes be contentious, difficult, perhaps even painful. But the crucial point is that such contention has to be based on a commitment to learning from a wealth of histories and experiences—*to more discussion, not less; to openness, not closure.*

This slide explains why I found the unionized faculty's response to be particularly interesting. On this slide is the letter of protest that was written in response to the dean's letter to the incoming students at the University of Chicago. Given that the faculty already had an opportunity to provide their input and have their concerns addressed, it is clearly dishonest of the signatories to this letter to now circulate a public grievance because they are unhappy with the decision. As we examine the contents of this letter, I hope that you will agree that it demonstrates that the letter was written by people who were unhappy with the

The Chicago Maroon

wealth of histories and experiences—*to more discussion, not less; to openness, not closure.*

The history of "safe spaces" goes back to gay, civil rights, and feminist efforts of the mid–20th century to create places protected from quite real forces of violence and intimidation. They also served as incubators of new ideas away from the censure of the very authorities threatened by these movements. It would be naïve to think that the University of Chicago is immune from social problems. Yet the administration confusingly disconnects "safe spaces" it supports (see the list of mentoring services on the College's own website) from "intellectual safe spaces" that it does not, as if issues of power and vulnerability stop at the classroom door.

The best spaces for independent thought and action may be those you create yourselves. For example, graduate student instructors at the University of Chicago have just won the right to organize as a labor union. We applaud their contributions to this national effort. Please see the statement of the University of Chicago chapter of the American Association of University Professors for further evidence of widespread faculty support of student activism and student rights.

The right to speak up and to make demands is at the very heart of academic freedom and freedom of expression generally. We deplore any atmosphere of harassment and threat. For just that reason, we encourage the Class of 2020 to speak up loudly and fearlessly.

Sincerely,

end result but who never considered the possibility that their ideas were not adopted because they failed to withstand scrutiny.

The last section of the letter stated that:

> The best spaces for independent thought and action may be those you create yourselves. For example, graduate student instructors at the University of Chicago have just won the right to organize as a labor union. We applaud their contributions to this national effort. Please see the statement of the University of Chicago chapter of the American Association of University Professors for further evidence of the widespread faculty support of student activism and student rights.

It is clear that the signatories to this letter disagreed with the University of Chicago's faculty report.

This letter first came out last August. Because I received news about what was happening at the University of Chicago from my feed on Facebook, I thought that this was a major news item. I expected the American Association of University Professors to communicate this news to CAUT (the Canadian Association of University Teachers), a body that claims to represent Canadian academics. I expected CAUT, in turn, to communicate this news to its members, which would include my union: the Acadia University Faculty Association, and that from there this would be an item of discussion within our union meetings. Because this never happened, I asked myself: "Why?"

A point to keep in mind is that the signatories to this letter were not all of the faculty at the University of Chicago, but only the members of the American Association of University Professors. The next point to keep in mind is that unionization is different in Canada than in the U.S. In the U.S., if you work in a unionized workforce, joining a union is optional, whereas in Canada it's mandatory. Thus, because I'm part of a unionized faculty, I have to be a member regardless of my personal wishes. I am still required to pay dues whether I want to or not, so that's a key issue here. This reference to widespread faculty support is specifically for this subgroup at the University of Chicago.

So what they are saying is that they oppose what is in the University of Chicago's principles. If that's what they oppose, we may wonder what it is that they support. The next statement is telling:

> The right to speak up and to make demands is at the very heart of academic freedom and freedom of expression generally. We deplore any atmosphere of harassment and threat. For that reason, we encourage the Class of 2020 to speak up loudly and fearlessly.

I find this rather compelling and ask myself: "Which one is more in line with the protestors going out with signs or the idea of civilized discussion and debate?" Interestingly, it was at a union meeting that I heard one professor say that "it's our job [as union members] to make demands and it's their job [as administrators] to give in to our demands," which is entirely consistent with the above statement.[43]

The previous slide explicitly states that you "do not have the freedom to threaten or harass others." But on this current slide, it says that "we deplore any atmosphere of harassment and threat," when that clearly is not what was said in

43 I did not say this during the talk, but the professor who made this statement was Geoffrey Whitehall (Department of Politics, Acadia University). Interestingly, Dr. Whitehall went on to serve as a faculty representative on Acadia University's Board of Governors.

the original statement. I think there is definitely a disconnect between what the union is arguing for and what the general faculty body is arguing for. So this might explain why the dean's letter and the "faculty's" response to it were never discussed within our own university.

Let's tie this in with what is happening here at Acadia. Over the time that I've been at this university, I've noticed there have been a number of people who quit going to the union meetings because they either found the meetings pointless or because they were shouted down. Others were kicked out and later told me that their statements were misrepresented. Some have commented that they feel that they have to turn off their critical thinking skills when they attend union meetings. I've also had some conversations with some longtime members and heard some of the statements that they have made offhand, including that they felt that the union was no longer what it used to be. One member said that the union used to be the place where members could talk about anything, and there was a strong sense of solidarity—until the union started getting heavily involved with the Canadian Association of University Teachers.[44]

44 I learned the full implications of this section of my talk the hard way and plan to go into these details in my third and final book in this series; the tentative title for that book is "Speaking Truth to Power."

Contributing Factors: Strands of an Intricate Web

- University
  - Shift in political ideology in the professoriate

I don't want to make any cause-and-effect inferences, but there definitely seems to be something awry here. Going through the process of preparing this talk prompted me to do lots of digging. One major change that has happened since I became an undergraduate in 1989[45] is that there has been a major shift in the political ideology of our professoriate.[46] Interestingly, the major changes that I have observed started when I became a student back in 1989.

45 Interestingly, 1989 is the year that the Berlin Wall fell.

46 Another major change is that academia started to become increasingly specialized in the 1990s. Because I have never raised this issue in any of the lectures that I have delivered or in any of my other writings, I will mention that a consequence of becoming increasingly specialized can be predicted by Mill's "He who knows" statement that I referenced earlier in the talk. Specifically, academics are now a group of people who have extensive knowledge within their narrow specialities that may or may not be based in truth, but have little to no understanding of how their knowledge relates to the bigger picture because they are largely unaware that a bigger picture even exists.

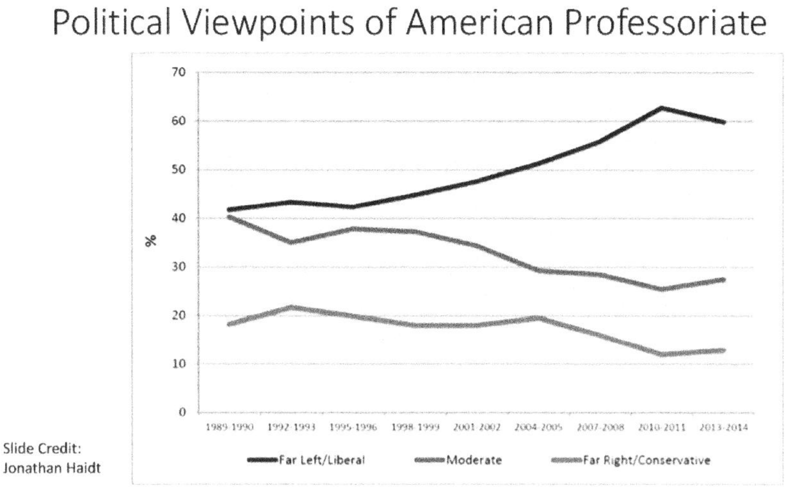

Back in 1989, the ratio of the far left and liberals versus the far right and conservatives was 2 to 1.[47] In 2013– 2014, the ratio was 6 to 1. However, depending on which part of the country you are in, the difference between these groups can be much larger. For example, in New England, the ratio of liberals to conservatives was 28 to 1.

This is an important issue because it seems clear that one's political orientation will affect the kind of research questions that will be asked, how the studies to answer those questions will be conducted, and how the data will be analyzed and interpreted.[48]

47 This study was done by Sam Abrams (Heterodox Academy).

48 A lesson that I have learned over the past few years is that the solution to this problem is to not have a political orientation. The ultimate problem with political orientations is that they are ideologies. Because ideologies cannot be refuted, they blind people to the truth. This explains why conversations with people who subscribe to an ideology are guaranteed to be unproductive; these people will not change their minds even if they are proven wrong.

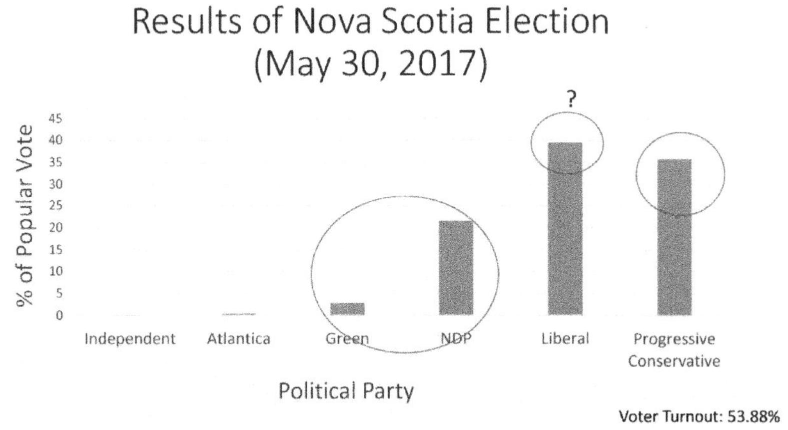

I don't have any data on the political orientation of the professoriate at Acadia and how it relates to the political orientation of the population, but I do have an idea of how we can test the hypothesis that the political orientation of our professoriate is different from that of the population of Nova Scotia. I would get a representative sample of our Acadia professoriate and ask them how they voted in the last provincial election that took place on May 30 of this year. I would then look at the distribution of how they voted in relation to how the population voted.

What I have here is the political party and the percent of the popular vote in the last provincial election. I would predict that we'd have an overrepresentation of the NDP and Green parties, collectively. In other words, these parties would be far overrepresented within the Acadia faculty. I would also expect to observe a large under-representation of the Progressive Conservative since it is very difficult to find people who are conservative on university campuses these days. As for the Liberals, I don't know what I would predict, which explains why I have a question mark on this portion of the slide.

In terms of why this is a concern, the university is starting to become irrelevant to the very society it is purporting to serve.[49]

49 This sentence turned out to be a major understatement.

Contributing Factors: Strands of an Intricate Web

- University
  - Shift in political ideology in the professoriate
    - Makeup not reflective of mainstream society
    - Power dynamics

When you have a group that is dominant, chances are they're not going to be benign in that position. Human nature being what it is, when a group is dominant like that, it is going to start to assert its power and we are starting to see evidence for power dynamics.

In 2010, one study reported by the American Association of Colleges and Universities found that only 17% of professors agreed that it was safe to hold unpopular views on campus.

Inbar & Lammers (2012), Study 2

- Sampled 266 members of Society for Personality and Social Psychology (SPSP)
  - Representative of overall membership on gender, age, nationality, and position
- Scale of hostile environment (1 = not at all, 4 = somewhat, 7 = very much)
  - How much they felt a hostile climate towards their political beliefs
  - Whether they were reluctant to express their political beliefs to their colleagues because they feared negative consequences
  - Whether they thought their colleagues would discriminate against them on the basis of their beliefs
  - Conservatives (4.7) > Moderates (3.7) > Liberal (1.9)

In this study from 2012, Inbar and Lammers sampled the membership of the Society for Personality and Social Psychology (SPSP). The sample they received was 266 members, which was representative of the Society as a whole on the variables gender, age, nationality, and position.

The sample was asked to rate, on a scale of 1 to 7, how hostile was their work environment, e.g., questions like whether they felt reluctant to express their political beliefs to their colleagues because they feared negative consequences. Interestingly, the conservatives gave a rating of about 5, the moderates around 4, and the liberals about 2. We can see that our conservative colleagues are afraid to speak their minds. Would there be a rationale for that? The answer from that study seems to be "yes."

Inbar & Lammers (2012), Study 2

Political Diversity in Social and Personality Psychology 501

Table 2. Stated Willingness to Discriminate Against Conservatives

	Self		Colleagues	
Item	*M (SD)*	Percentage of responses ≥4	*M (SD)*	Percentage of responses ≥4
Paper review	2.4 (1.3)	18.6	3.0 (1.5)	34.2
Grant review	2.5 (1.3)	23.8	3.0 (1.5)	36.9
Symposium invite	2.1 (1.3)	14.0	2.7 (1.5)	29.6
Hiring decision	2.9 (1.7)	37.5	3.4 (1.7)	44.1

Note. All ratings were on scales from 1 (*Not at all*) to 7 (*Very much*), with the midpoint labeled 4 (*Somewhat*). All means differ significantly from 1 ($ps < .001$).

As part of their study, the authors asked people if they were willing to discriminate against a conservative colleague in the context of reviewing a paper, e.g., "Are you willing to reject them if you know that they are conservative?" The percentages that were willing to do this were: roughly 25% in the context of a grant review, 15% in the context of inviting them to give a talk, and almost 40% in the context of hiring. We can see that there is clear discrimination with respect to deciding people's careers.

In terms of power dynamics, we have a professoriate that consists almost exclusively of liberals and the far left. A moderate liberal will be okay with making a change to society as long as the evidence is there to warrant it, but those on the far left are going to find oppression no matter where they look. In the short term, their target is going to be their conservative colleagues. But once there are no more conservatives on college campuses, then by definition the natural target for the far left will be the liberals.

In other words, when you have this major case of groupthink, which is the situation in every college, the left is going to eat itself. And that's a big danger that we all have to worry about.

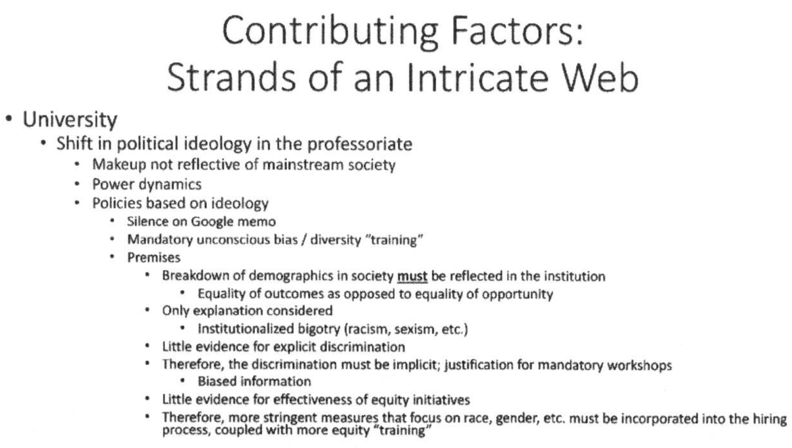

When you have a groupthink dynamic, it will be reflected in the policies that are implemented. Interestingly, we had the Google memo issue this summer, and all the reports I read in the media seem to say that the person who wrote the Google memo [James Damore] was, for the most part, scientifically accurate. So there was nothing of contention there, but there seemed to be a complete silence on university campuses about that issue, and that always struck me as odd.

A policy that is strongly endorsed these days is mandatory unconscious bias and diversity "training." [50] I put the word "training" in quotation marks because it's not really "training" that you receive, and it's not like you acquired a skill set that you didn't have before. The rationale for this "training" is that we must break down society into its demographics and that the percentages in the population HAVE to be reflected at the institution.

There is a distinction between equality of outcomes and equality of opportunity. Equality of opportunity means that if you apply for a job and you have the skills, we are not going to take into consideration issues that are irrelevant to your ability to do your job, such as race or gender. However, with equality of outcomes, we are required to take into consideration issues that are irrelevant to your ability to do your job so that the percentages at our institution are the same as those as society at large.

What is interesting about this issue is that my colleagues who generally are rational when I discuss other issues with them respond that "it has to be this

50 The terms "implicit bias" and "unconscious bias" are often used interchangeably. In a similar vein, the terms "equity training" and "diversity training" are often used interchangeably.

way" when I question them about equity; they respond that the issue cannot be discussed further.[51] I do not understand the disconnect between how one can be rational on all issues other than this one.

So now we have this idea in place that a distribution that is present in the public must also be reflected in the institution and that the only explanation for a discrepancy that can be considered is some form of institutionalized bigotry like racism, sexism, or homophobia. In addition, these labels are used against those who ask questions.

Interestingly, people who are liberally minded would typically be opposed to any form of discrimination in the first place. Since we cannot find any evidence for an explicit form of discrimination, the assumption is that the discrimination must somehow be implicit. This then becomes the justification for these mandatory workshops.

Having attended these mandatory workshops, I can tell you that completely biased information is presented as if it is the consensus.

The next question that we can ask ourselves is whether these workshops are effective. Unfortunately, there's little evidence that they work.[52] If you ask people to participate in equity surveys voluntarily, the maximum participation rate is 40%, with 5% of people saying they do not want to answer; so there's not much of an intake; in other words, there is little evidence of the membership being interested in these surveys and workshops. It certainly is not something that is being demanded by the membership. Instead, this is something that comes more from above.

Thus, we cannot determine whether these workshops are effective or not since we do not have any data proving that these techniques work. If anything, the fact that we haven't reached equal outcomes despite these workshops should be interpreted as evidence that these techniques do not work.

But instead of abandoning a bad idea, the powers that be have decided that they need to focus more stringently on incorporating race and gender into our hiring process. This reinforces the idea that we must have more equity training.

Given that the advocates for these measures have presented their argument in such black-and-white terms, it is going to take very little to counter their stance.

51 I did not name the colleagues that I had in mind when I made this comment during my lecture, but the ones that I had in mind were Dr. Karmen Bleile (a colleague in the Department of Psychology) and Dr. Glenys Gibson (a colleague in the Department of Biology). Both of these individuals, interestingly enough, are members of WISE (Women in Science and Engineering.

52 The data that I am reporting here are the participation rates in surveys administered by the Acadia University Faculty Association.

PNAS

National hiring experiments reveal 2:1 faculty preference for women on STEM tenure track

Wendy M. Williams[1] and Stephen J. Ceci

Department of Human Development, Cornell University, Ithaca, NY 14853

Edited* by Richard E. Nisbett, University of Michigan, Ann Arbor, MI, and approved March 5, 2015 (received for review September :

"Applicants' profiles were systematically varied to disguise identically rated scholarship... Results revealed a 2:1 preference for women by faculty of both genders across both math-intensive and non–math-intensive fields, with the single exception of male economists, who showed no gender preference."

Slide Credit: Jonathan Haidt

This is a study looking at the field of STEM. This was a real experiment[53] in which the authors gave researchers in various disciplines profiles of job applicants who were either men or women and asked the researchers who they would hire. There was a much stronger preference for women over men. It was a 2-to-1 preference. This demonstrates that there is discrimination and that it's actually discrimination against men, not women. This response was across both genders, so it didn't matter if it was a male doing the reviewing or a female. Williams and Ceci also saw this trend across fields; the only exception were male economists who did not show a gender preference one way or another. The authors have concluded that this is a good time for women to be going into STEM and that it is not all doom and gloom.

These data fly in the face of the premise of institutionalized sexism.

53 In a real experiment, people are randomly assigned to their conditions, e.g., they have an equal chance of being assigned to an experimental group and a control group. Random assignment is a technique that is used to help ensure that the groups are similar on characteristics that are irrelevant to the study (e.g., if height is an issue, then random assignment helps to ensure that the two groups have similar heights as opposed to all of the tall people being in one group and all of the short people being in the other group). This technique minimizes the chances that factors that are outside of the researcher's control can explain the results of the experiment.

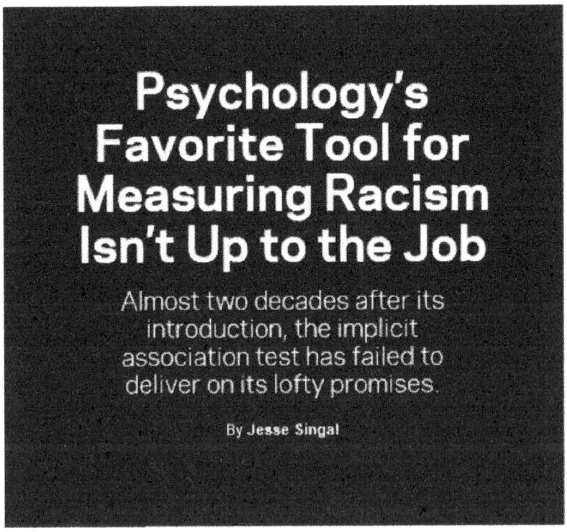

Psychology's Favorite Tool for Measuring Racism Isn't Up to the Job

Almost two decades after its introduction, the implicit association test has failed to deliver on its lofty promises.

By Jesse Singal

At equity seminars, the attendees are told that implicit bias and stereotype threat explain unequal outcomes. There are problems with the literature on both constructs. For instance, in implicit bias research, participants are asked to classify people as, let's say, "lazy" versus "hardworking". So if you put someone black under "lazy" rather than "hardworking," the conclusion is that the person must be racist, even if the participant who responded this way happened to be black. The other alternative that makes more sense is that most of us are familiar with the stereotype of a black person being lazy. Thus, familiarity as opposed to hatred or fear can explain the results in this line of research.

An additional problem is that the only other data that the researchers have to work with are reaction times, but they have no way of knowing what went into a person's reaction time.

There are also two other problems that we see in both the implicit bias and stereotype threat literatures: small effect sizes and failure to replicate; e.g., when the effect that the researcher is looking for happens to be small, it often does not replicate.

The third problem is known as "publication bias," meaning that researchers are more likely to get their research published if they report one set of results than if they report other types of results.[54] Regarding the issue of implicit bias, a recent article by Jesse Singal says that maybe it's time to put this measure away since it's probably well past its best-before date.

54 I would later be proven right when the "Grievance Hoax Studies" was published in 2018 (Lindsay, J.A., Boghossian, P., & Pluckrose, H. (2018)). Academic Grievance Studies and the Corruption of Scholarship *(Aero Magazine)*.

Stereotype Threat?

Female chess players outperform expectations when playing men

Tom Stafford
Department of Psychology, University of Sheffield
Sheffield, S1 2LT, United Kingdom

"Stereotype threat" has been offered as a potential explanation of differential performance between men and women in some cognitive domains. Questions remain about the reliability and generality of the phenomenon. Previous studies have found that stereotype threat is activated in female chess players when they are matched against male players. I use data from over 5.5 million games of international tournament chess and find no evidence of a stereotype threat effect. In fact women players outperform expectations when playing men. Further analysis shows no influence of degree of challenge, nor of player age, nor of prevalence of female role models in national chess leagues on differences in performance when women play men versus when they play women. Though this analysis contradicts one specific mechanism of influence of gender stereotypes, the persistent differences between male and female players suggest that systematic factors do exist and remain to be uncovered.

Now let's turn to stereotype threat.

Stereotype threat is the notion that visible minorities will perform worse on an exam if they are given cues that call attention to their visible minority status than if they are given cues that do not call attention to their visible minority status. The general idea is that people who are from minority groups will perform worse if they are given cues that heighten their feelings about their status. A rather obvious alternative explanation for this result is "demand characteristics," which means that the participants have figured out the researcher's hypothesis and are changing their responses so that they are either in line with or disconfirm the hypothesis. Demand characteristics are another factor that can explain why the results in this area are mixed.

I recently came across a study that's soon to appear in *Psychological Science* that I believe decimates the idea of stereotype threat. Rather than being worse than men at chess, this researcher found that female chess players are much better than men: "I used data from over 5.5 million games of international tournament chess and found no evidence of a stereotype threat effect."

I think the data I have presented demonstrate that there is no basis for the problems that we are trying to solve.

Potential Solutions: Acadia Taking Action

- Ask questions to both the union and the Board
    - Students
    - Faculty

In our current round of collective bargaining, we're at the stage where we're going into conciliation and a possible strike vote. For students, that's definitely something you need to worry about. I think this is a good time to start asking pointed questions of both the union and the board, such as: "Why are we pursuing these kinds of policies when the evidence for them is rather weak?"

Earlier in this talk, I mentioned an open letter that I sent to the Acadia community in which I asked pointed questions. One problem was that the union's membership filled out an online survey that contained biased multiple choice questions. When it came to the written section, we had no way of knowing whether the results were analyzed objectively or whether they were reported with a clear lens. Within the union meetings, I have been trying repeatedly to propose alternatives, but to no avail.

If you're a student, I think this is the time to ask really pointed questions from both sides, such as why are union members advocating for a strike.

THE WALL STREET JOURNAL.

OPINION | COMMENTARY

Mizzou Pays a Price for Appeasing the Left

Enrollment is down more than 2,000. The campus has had to take seven dormitories out of service

By Jillian Kay Melchior
Aug. 20, 2017 3:48 p.m. ET

In terms of where we (as a society) are going and why I am so strongly opposed to these measures that are being adopted by our universities, it is clear that we have a group of extremists that are attempting to take over the campuses. They will go to extreme lengths to search for examples of "oppression" and don't care about the costs of their actions.

This slide shows a scene from a protest that happened at the University of Missouri, where a professor walks up to a student with a camera and says, "You need to leave now" and "I'm going to need some muscle around here." This incident happened in October 2015, and the person in the photo is Professor Melissa Click.

Fast forward to August 2017. Their first-year enrollment is down 35% since those protests. They now have seven dorms that have been closed, and in May they announced they would lay off 100 people and eliminate 300 more positions through retirement and attrition. Last year, they also reduced their library staff and their clean management jobs by 50 positions. The most affected are the ones who are the lowest paid and are the most vulnerable.

Evergreen State College: Background Information

Bret Weinstein, Biology

George Bridges, President

Now I'll discuss what happened at Evergreen State College earlier this summer. There are many key players in this case, but I'll focus on a couple. One was Bret Weinstein, who was a professor of biology, and the other was the president, George Bridges. When Bridges arrived, he decided that the college was going to implement an Employment Equity initiative across the university. This was something that Bret Weinstein strongly opposed.

Evergreen State College: Background Information

- Weinstein called a racist for raising concerns about equity proposals
- Hardline Approach to Equity, Diversity, & Inclusion [see videos by Benjamin A. Boyce]: Allies or Enemies
  - "Bring 'em in, train 'em, and if they don't get it, sanction 'em"
    - George Bridges to students

  Other comments
  - "Threats to equity must be eliminated"
  - "We're inviting you to come along. We're going to do it. Don't get it twisted, but we would like for you to join us"
  - "Unscrew institutional racism"
- Day of Absence / Day of Presence

When he raised concerns about this, he was labeled a racist and a white supremacist, while others stayed silent.

Benjamin Boyce is a former poet who decided to become a YouTube critic. He has been digging into what has happened at Evergreen by using tools such as the Freedom of Information and Privacy Act. He also discovered some rather disturbing recordings.

This is what the president said to students: "Bring 'em in, train 'em, and if they don't get it, sanction 'em" when it pertained to the issue of employment equity. Other statements made by faculty members include:

> "Threats to equity must be eliminated."
>
> "Unscrew institutional racism."
>
> "We're inviting you to come along. We're going to do it. Don't get it twisted, but we would like for you to join us."

This gives you a flavour of what was happening on the campus two years prior to this summer's incident.

What led to the events of May involved a tradition at Evergreen State College called the Day of Absence or Day of Presence. This involved the visible minorities leaving the campus for a day, which was their way of showing what happens when they're not around and how they matter. This particular year, the director of the First Peoples Multicultural Advisory Services demanded that white people leave the campus for the day. Bret Weinstein then sent an email in which he stated that there is a difference between one group voluntarily absenting themselves and another group being demanded to leave for the day. He also stated that we should not go on the basis of our phenotype; we should not go on the basis of our skin colour. The day passed uneventfully, but fast forward to May 23rd, the students realized they should make whatever point they wished to make because the term was ending soon.

WRITING CENTER

The visual images on this slide speak volumes. Bret Weinstein was lecturing. Suddenly, 50 people were outside of his class. He came out and attempted to have a discussion with them. In this discussion, he asked them if they would like to hear his answer, and their response was "no."

Later in the day, a group of about 100 students headed to the president's office and the library. Some of the things that transpired involved the students saying, "We have pizza here, but it's for people of colour only."

At one point, the president was speaking normally, just the way I am, and people screamed out "microaggressions" and told him to "stand like this," with their arms by their sides. He wanted to go to the washroom, and he needed to be chaperoned for that.

After that, things got out of control, and the school closed for three full days.

Bret Weinstein
@BretWeinstein
Follow

The President @EvergreenStCol is barricaded w/ protestors. Police forced to stand down by Pres campus under protest-control. Students Unsafe

7:00 PM - 24 May 2017

100 Retweets 128 Likes

22 100 128

Bret Weinstein @BretWeinstein · May 24
Replying to
The press is MIA. College papering over the problem, putting students, staff + faculty at risk. Police have given me an unambiguous warning

15 73 170

Bret Weinstein @BretWeinstein · May 24
To be clear: the police told me i am not safe on campus. They can not protect me. Students in jeopardy. No contact from admin. George?

28 111 232

Bret Weinstein
@BretWeinstein
Follow

My students are being singled out for disagreeing with the conventional wisdom. Witch hunt, 2017. @EvergreenStCol is silent on the matter.

i have names and faces of students in bret's class who were filming the class protest yesterday and who are actively defending him, if you would like to see these faces for your own safety, please contact me or message me on here

Seen by 50

Like Comment

12:10 AM - 25 May 2017

758 Retweets 1,260 Likes

121 758 1.3K

Naima Niambi
5 hrs

Oh lord,
Could some white women at Evergreen come and collect Heather Heying's racist ass.
Jesus

Like Comment Share

I think the tweets speak volumes about what was happening that day. Bret Weinstein tweeted that the "police were forced to stand down by the president." The president told the police not to do anything. The campus was unsafe. His wife expressed concerns that her husband is unsafe, and this was the response from the director of the Equity Council: "Oh Lord, could some white women at Evergreen come and collect Heather Heying's racist ass [Heather Heying is Bret Weinstein's wife]?" Some of the students who were on Weinstein's side ended up being doxed.

This is definitely not an image that we want for our campus, in which students with baseball bats call the shots.

The tweets speak to the utter mayhem. Bret Weinstein's brother, Eric Weinstein, said that "I never once in a million years dreamed that Fox would be the voice of reason." It was curious that the liberal media was rather silent; it took them three weeks before they sent anyone to the campus to get coverage of this. This situation was completely surreal.

Evergreen State College: Meeting with Board of Trustees (July 12, 2017)

McKenzie Kyger

Fast forward to a meeting of Evergreen's Board of Trustees in July 2017, where only two people spoke out to say that what happened was utterly wrong. One was Bret Weinstein, the target of the protest. The other was the only student who spoke out, McKenzie Kyger, who said that we are now so obsessed with race that we are becoming racist here.

Evergreen State College:
Meeting with Board of Trustees (July 12, 2017)

Everyone else thought this was a great idea and that they may not have gone far enough. This is the groupthink mentality. These are the people who espouse the values of equity or diversity repeatedly and speak about anti-oppression and how we must encourage it.

See other videos from Badger Pundit YouTube Page

Listed in the Reference Section

If you are interested in knowing more about what happened at Evergreen State College, you should also check out Badger Pundit's YouTube page. There are many interesting videos there.

Rep. Matt Manweller aims to cut Evergreen off from state

BY MYNORTHWEST.COM
JUNE 8, 2017 AT 9:48 PM

Share

State Rep. Matt Manweller represents Washington's 13th District. (Washington House Republicans)

Enrollment At Evergreen State College Drops 5%, Hiring Freeze To Follow

JOHN SEXTON Posted at 7:41 pm on September 1, 2017

SHARE ON FACEBOOK SHARE ON TWITTER 61

After the events, one of the people who was a professor at the university and is now in the legislature (Representative Matt Mannweller) is saying that it's time to cut funds to the university. The general idea is that it should become a private university that focuses solely on STEM; in other words, disregard the arts.[55]

55 I disagree with this idea because I believe that a well-rounded education includes exposure to the arts.

Thanks in part to the events that transpired in May, Evergreen now has a $2.1 million budget deficit. They already had declining enrollment to begin with, but this fiasco accelerated that decline further.

What was really bizarre is that after mentioning the hiring freeze, the university published the following statements in their budget document:

1) "We must continue our efforts to make Evergreen a student-ready college."
2) "Our work in equity and inclusion is an important step in this process."

This is what they are putting in their own documentation. Despite everything that had happened, they thought this was a great idea and that they must somehow continue on this path.[56]

56 Although I did not say these words, I did use a tone in which I tried to communicate the point that "you can't fix stupid."

Potential Solutions: Addressing Hate

At this point, it would be a good idea for us to maybe close our eyes and take one or two deep breaths.[57]

In terms of where I want to go from here: Whatever happens, I do NOT want you to think about a pink elephant. Did you notice that you immediately thought about a pink elephant after I told you to not do that? [The audience nodded their heads up and down.]

The answer appears to be a resounding "yes," which is what one would expect. That's step one.

Now I will tell you a story, which I believe is from the Cherokee First Nations tradition:

> A grandfather is talking with this grandson and he says that "there are two wolves inside each of us which are always at war with each other. One of them is the good wolf that represents things like kindness, bravery, and love; the other is a bad wolf, which represents greed, hatred, and fear."
>
> The grandson stops and thinks for a second and then looks up at the grandfather and asks, "Well, grandfather, which one wins?" And the grandfather quietly responds, "The one you feed."

Instead of addressing "hate speech," we should be addressing "hate."

The lesson from the thought experiment[58] and story is that the more you try to suppress hate directly, the stronger it gets. The same thing happens with chronic pain. When people have chronic pain and we try to fight the pain, the stronger it gets; this explains why we use techniques such as relaxation training, biofeedback, and meditation to treat people suffering from chronic pain. The

57 I did this because I could feel the tension in the room and thought that now was the time to end the talk on a more inspirational note.

58 The thought experiment demonstrated a psychological phenomenon known as "thought suppression."

question of concern for the patients is: "How do we live with this unwelcome guest that's living inside our body?" The answer is: Instead of trying to suppress the beast that lives within us, we should be feeding the angels that live inside of all of us.[59]

This is hardly anything new. Anyone who has taken a first-year psychology course knows that you're better off using positive reinforcement to develop the behaviours that you want than trying to suppress the ones that you don't want. This is the basis of positive psychology and humanism. It's hardly reinventing the wheel.

59 At the time, I had no idea that I was referring to Biblical principles in this section of my talk, and I did not understand that my references to Biblical principles explained why my colleagues hated me. I now understand what Jesus Christ meant when He said that the world hates Him because they hate the one who sent Him (our Father) and what He meant when He said that no servant outperforms the master, i.e., that my love for His values guaranteed that my colleagues would hate and persecute me.

Daryl Davis: Accidental Courtesy

There are also some inspiring real-life stories that show that this approach works. The gentleman in this photo goes by the name of Daryl Davis. He was interested in the following question regarding white supremacy: "Why is it that you hate me when you don't even know me?" To answer this question, he introduced himself to white supremacists and soon became friends with them. His secret to success was that he could find common ground with anyone within five minutes. He would focus on the commonalities first. Over time, he noticed that he could form and build a bond with the person who he thought was his enemy, and that eventually he and the white supremacists saw each other as human beings.

What makes him notable is that roughly two hundred members of the KKK have given up their robes. You can watch this in the documentary called "Accidental Courtesy," which can be watched on places such as Netflix.

The Inquirer
DAILY NEWS philly.com

NEWS SPORTS BUSINESS HEALTH ENTERTAINMENT FOOD OPINION REAL ESTATE OBITS Log In

Already a print subscriber? **Get Access** Already a digital subscriber? **Log In** Never Miss a Story **Subscribe Today**

Viewpoints

In Lower Merion, Democrats and Republicans try something new: Listening to each other

Updated: AUGUST 25, 2017 — 8:57 AM EDT

© DAVID MAIALETTI / STAFF PHOTOGRAPHER
'Hate Has No Home Here' signs have appeared since Election Day, and one community had a discussion about their impact

by **Ashley Best-Raiten**

Given the intensity of the 2016 American election, there are people who are trying to heal and unite after an extended period of division. One way that some towns are doing this is by getting together as a community for the purpose of fostering communication.

This article describes how one town organized sessions in which one half of people would talk about their experiences of what happened in the election while the other half would sit there and listen. The second group agreed to not to have any reaction whatsoever, not so much as an eyeroll, while the other side talked. The two sides then switched roles.

The idea here is that some of the small towns in the US are taking time to heal and to get to know each other as human beings.

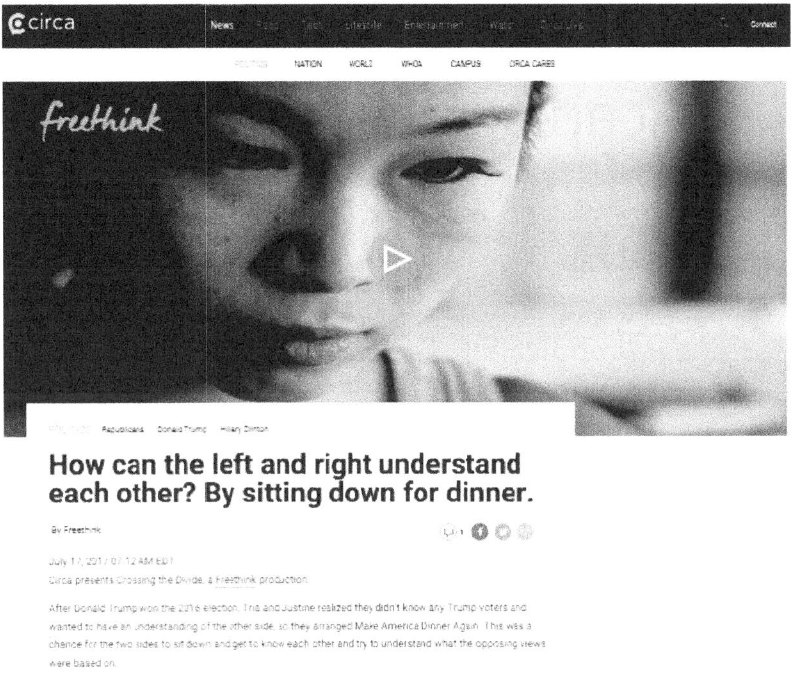
circa
News
Connect
NATION WORLD WHOA CAMPUS CIRCA CARES
freethink
Republicans Donald Trump Hillary Clinton

How can the left and right understand each other? By sitting down for dinner.

By Freethink

July 17, 2017 07:12 AM EDT

Circa presents Crossing the Divide, a Freethink production

After Donald Trump won the 2016 election, Tria and Justine realized they didn't know any Trump voters and wanted to have an understanding of the other side, so they arranged Make America Dinner Again. This was a chance for the two sides to sit down and get to know each other and try to understand what the opposing views were based on.

We are seeing this same kind of thing in some of the big cities. In this case, two women—Tri and Justine—decided to create a context in which they could bring people together. They called their initiative "Make America Dinner Again." As a foodie and punster, I quite endorse this one.

The key point is that people are rediscovering the secrets to happiness and to creating a truly positive social change.

Potential Solutions: Acadia Taking Action

In the spirit of Ruth Simmons and the Students for Free Expression (Kudos to Matthew Foldi)

What I'm proposing here is in the spirit of Ruth Simmons. There's also a student group on Facebook that you can check out called "Students for Free Expression." That group is headed by Matthew Foldi.

For the first proposal, I am hoping that the student groups will take the lead on this because I clearly have a vested interest in this issue. What we need is someone who is independent of me so that we don't need to worry about conflicts of interest. The idea behind this proposal is to initiate a conversation with students about how comfortable they feel expressing their views. The main idea is that everyone has a voice in this process, but that no one can take it over. I thus propose that the ASU [Acadia Students' Union] form the committee that does this research; they can decide which faculty members and students to include on this committee. Is Samantha here today?[60]

60 During my talk, I asked if the Vice President Academic for the Acadia Students' Union was in attendance because she would have been the logical student representative to pursue this questioning. Interestingly, the Vice President Academic (Samantha Nixon) did not attend a talk that was directly relevant to her job: A clear case of dereliction of duty on her part.

Potential Solutions: Acadia Taking Action

Abandon commitment to social justice

- Treat activism and scholarship with the same caution as business and scholarship
- Reaffirm commitment to truth, but include as many perspectives as possible

Heterodox Academy

- Make a formal commitment to viewpoint diversity
  - Implement a policy that explicitly states that student groups will not be charged security fees
  - Implement a policy on how to deal with controversial speakers
- Adopt the Chicago Principles on Freedom of Expression
- Academic freedom for all (i.e., staff included)
- Institutionalized disconfirmation
  - Example: ask about tolerance of viewpoint diversity when interviewing candidates
  - Use Harrison McCain Research Award to encourage collaborations across opposing viewpoints
- Focus on purpose of speech (e.g., why, what) → encourage more speech, rather than less

One key problem with our university is its commitment to social justice. The situation at Acadia University is so bad that the only type of coffee available at this campus is fair trade coffee, which means that our institution is one where you can quite literally have social justice rammed down your throat.[61]

We need to abandon this commitment to social justice and treat activism the same way we would treat a corporation. In the same way that we need to ensure that corporations don't dictate our university's decisions, we also need to ensure that activists don't dictate our university's decisions.[62] Our goal as an institution should still be the pursuit of the truth. I have no problem with activists having their voices heard, as long as no one is allowed to dominate a conversation. In essence, I am proposing that we increase the size of the table because this will give more people the opportunity to be at the table and to have their voices heard. This is in contrast to excluding anyone.

The next set of ideas is inspired by the Heterodox Academy, a group of academics who are advocating for viewpoint diversity on college campuses. In addition to abandoning our commitment to social justice, I propose that we make a formal commitment to viewpoint diversity, given that this is key to seeking truth.

I'm recommending that our university implement a policy that explicitly states that student groups are not going to be charged security fees if they're

61 I noticed that Grace Hamilton-Burge's (President, Acadia Students' Union) jaw dropped when I made this comment. I will explain the significance of her action later in this book.

62 When I made this comment, I had only a superficial understanding of how much corporations dictate our universities' curricula.

going to be bringing in controversial speakers. At a more general level, we should have a policy in place that deals with the issue of controversial speakers. The idea here is that people who are opposed to the speaker have a forum in which their voices are heard. This way, they can have a platform where they can voice their concerns; this is far better than shouting a speaker down.

Earlier in this talk, I mentioned the University of Chicago's principles on academic freedom and expression; adopting these principles is one of my suggestions. At this stage, only faculty members and students have academic freedom. Rather than granting academic freedom to only a select group of people at our campuses, I am advocating for academic freedom for everyone at our campuses, including staff and visitors.

One of the principles that the Heterodox Academy advocates for is institutionalized disconfirmation. The idea here is that if you are interviewing a job candidate, you can ask them to give an example of when they have exhibited tolerance for someone who has a very different point of view from them. That could be one example.

A strategy that I have come up with is based on what the Heterodox Academy did, which was to have liberal professors work with the American Enterprise Institute on a research project. At Acadia University, one of the research awards that we have is the Harrison McCain Research Award. And earlier in the talk, I mentioned that a criticism of Canada's budget is that it ignored the needs of men and that this has caused needless tension between the sexes. A logical solution to this problem is to have a research collaboration in which people with different points of view come together to work on a problem as equals in order to serve a greater good. The people in the group would benefit because they are focused on solving a problem rather on their differences with others in the group. I thus propose that the Women's and Gender Studies Department and the Department of Economics work with the Canadian Association for Equality on a budget that is truly a gender-balanced budget.

Interestingly, the Canadian Association for Equality is sometimes given a bad rap because of its reputation as a men's rights group, and feminists are often written off as man-haters. By collaborating on a project that serves a greater good, especially when it involves working with a men's rights group, feminists would be able to show the public that they are not man-haters.[63]

When it comes to the idea of speech, instead of finding reasons to shut it down, we should be finding ways to encourage dialogue. One way that we can do this is by focusing on the purpose of the speech. When someone makes a comment with which we disagree, we can follow up by asking that person

63 The fact that none of the feminists at Acadia University took me up on this offer speaks volumes about the content of their character.

questions such as “Why are you saying that?” and “What do you hope to achieve here?”

The point, once again, is not to suppress free speech but to guide speakers and listeners so that they engage in conversations that are productive. This approach emphasizes the importance of keeping lines of dialogue open. Even if we disagree now, as long as we’re able to keep the lines of communication open and keep talking, we will have the opportunity to reach common ground.

Potential Solutions: Acadia Taking Action

- Assertiveness training and debating workshops
  - Empower students to express and defend their views
  - Learn the art of overcoming bad ideas with good ones, instead of shutting people down (e.g., because of being offended)
- Broader conversations
  - Are we losing our humanity when we focus so much on our identity?
  - Can we do a better job of working collectively as a community to attain our shared goals while still maintaining our individuality?

One thing I have noticed over the course of my lifetime is that the art of conversation and debate seems to have gone by the wayside. To address this problem, we could have workshops for students on how to assert themselves in a classroom setting. Within the context of assertiveness training, we can also teach students how to debate. This training would not only empower students by teaching them how to defend their views, but will also benefit them in other areas of their lives.

Lastly, instead of teaching our students to label a person or idea with which they disagree as racist or sexist and to then use the label as a pretext for shutting people down, we would be better off teaching our students how to overcome bad ideas by proposing good ideas.

I will close this talk by asking questions that I hope will be the basis for ongoing and broad conversations within our community:

1) When we focus on our differences, do we lose out on our common goals? In other words, are we losing our humanity when we focus on identity politics?
2) Can we do a better job of working collectively as a community to work on our shared goals while at the same time maintaining our individuality?

On this note, I thank you for your time.

Aftermath

"People generally see what they look for, and hear what they listen for."

"It's never an insult to be called what somebody thinks is a bad name. It just shows you how poor that person is, it doesn't hurt you."

—Harper Lee, *To Kill a Mockingbird*

September 27, 2017

I had no idea what to expect when I delivered my talk and was frightened at the thought that protestors might assault me. For these reasons, I spent much of the day feeling nervous and anxious. Thankfully, I was able to hide my fear when I delivered my talk that evening. From what I can tell, the only telltale sign of my stress was the fact that I consumed a large bottle of water during my talk. This is highly unusual because I normally do not consume fluids when I deliver lectures.

The audience consisted of 46 to 50 people, the vast majority of whom were students. The only faculty members who showed up were 3 of my opponents,[64] and it was clear that they came for the purpose of asking me rude and aggressive questions at the end of my talk instead of asking me about issues related to the substance of my talk, i.e., the questions and comments consisted of personal attacks.

During my talk, I noticed that there was little evidence of boredom in the audience, i.e., people normally fidget or text incessantly during a lecture if it is not engaging. On the contrary, I noticed that people's jaws would drop from time to time. When I had finished my talk, I looked at the clock and was shocked to discover that I had been speaking for an hour and forty-five minutes. Because I knew that I would not want to listen to myself speak for that long, I was amazed that anyone else would want to listen to me for that long.

One incident during my talk that stood out to me was the moment that Grace Hamilton-Burge's (President, Acadia Students' Union) jaw dropped. For context, at that point in the talk, I criticized the university's administration for their incredibly stupid decision of making fair trade coffee the only coffee option available on campus. I later found out that it was Ms. Hamilton-Burge's idea, as opposed to the administration's idea, to make fair trade coffee the only available option for coffee that was sold by the Acadia Students' Union; apparently, the university administration thought this idea was so good that it should be adopted across the campus.

Another incident that stood out to me happened near the end of the evening. After the question and answer period was over, I was about to announce that

64 One of the professors was Jeff Sachs (Department of Politics). Dr. Sachs attended with his wife, Erin Crandall, who happens to be a professor in the Department of Politics and is associated with Acadia's Women's and Gender Studies program. Interestingly, Dr. Sachs was also rude and aggressive in his line of questioning at the free speech panel discussion that I had organized in May 2017. The third professor was Eva Curry (Department of Mathematics and Statistics), who also happens to be a member of Women in Science and Engineering (WISE) at Acadia. Interestingly, she too conducted herself unprofessionally at the free speech panel discussion that I organized in May 2017.

I was willing to stay to talk to anyone who wanted to talk to me. But before I could do that, Sid Kondapuram (editor-in-chief, The Athenaeum) announced that everyone had to leave the room because he had booked the room only until 8:30 p.m. The fact of the matter, though, is that the custodians do not clean the classrooms until after 10 p.m. His action here confirmed my suspicion that he was working against me, albeit quietly at this stage.

Because I was high strung for most of the day, I was emotionally drained and exhausted after I had delivered my talk. However, my spirits were lifted when I saw a message that I had received at 10:50 p.m. from Mackenzie O'Quinn, a student who had never taken a course with me, with the subject heading "THANK YOU".[65] Below is a copy of the email message that he sent me:

Dr. Mehta,

I attended your talk tonight and honestly I was in awe the entire time. I want to commend you on your courage and your absolute honesty in speaking the truth in and to an institution that would rather not hear it, as was seen in the arguments at the end.

I found your talk incredibly enlightening, and I am grateful for everything you said, because I personally have felt uncomfortable sharing my views within class and throughout this institution as a whole. I have also been verbally attacked just for opening mildly controversial discussions in class, which is problematic in an environment literally dedicated to uncovering truth and learning about reality. If we can't talk about these issues here, where should they be talked about?

As well, I am so incredibly grateful that you mentioned science being ignored and the whole "there is no place for science in this" narrative that is all too common today. As a double major student in Biology and Sociology, I find too often that scientific fact is blatantly ignored by individuals when it suits their argument. In fact, even here at Acadia I had a conversation with a member of the Sociology faculty about research that had been done on the harmful effects of pornography on the brain, its chemistry, and within social relationships, and I was shut down. The comment was "science has no place in Sociology and in fact is

65 The first comment that I will make is that I am deeply grateful for Mr. O'Quinn's kind and thoughtful email message. The second comment is that, until I received his email message, I did not know that research had been done that demonstrates that pornography can damage brain functioning.

more problematic". That statement has stuck with me and I am glad that you gave voice to it tonight.

In conclusion, I am grateful to you for speaking to a truth about censorship and the suppression of free speech in universities that I experience daily. I am glad that I am not the only one concerned about the way things are going. You did a fantastic job, and I am excited to see where the conversation goes from here.

Thanks,

Mr. Makenzie O'Quinn
2nd year Biology/Sociology
Acadia University

October 4, 2017

At 10:34 p.m. on Wednesday, October 4, 2017, I sent an email message to Acadia University's faculty and staff with the heading "Slides, References, and Audio Link for My Talk (Free Speech in Universities: Threats and Opportunities)" and in which I circulated not only the slides and reference section for my talk,[66] but also a link to an audio recording of the talk while I was waiting for my video recording to be ready. The purpose of this message was to generate a discussion about my talk. Below is a copy of the email message that I had sent:

Good Morning Acadia Community,

I was hoping to attach the slides and a list of all of the sources that I had reviewed to prepare the talk that I delivered on the evening of Wednesday, September 27 at 7 p.m., which was titled "Free Speech in Universities: Threats and Opportunities." Because the files are too large for the university's server, I'm instead placing a link to my Dropbox account, where people should be able to download these materials: https://db.tt/GMihoeg7L9[67] I was also hoping to send out a link to a video recording of my talk, but unfortunately, the video is not ready yet. However, Axe Radio livestreamed my talk and archived it. For those who are interested in listening to the talk as a podcast while waiting for the video to come out, please go to https://www.mixcloud.com/AxeRadio2017/free-speech-in-universities-with-rick-mehta/.[68] Because I was covering a lot of ground, my talk was longer than I had anticipated (it was roughly 1:45, when I thought it would be 1:15), but, much to my surprise, most of the audience stayed for the whole talk. I hope that the length of the talk won't be a deterrent.

Before the talk, I sent out an outline so that the community would have a general idea of what to expect with regard to the content, but I tried to avoid giving away any of the specific points that I

66 The reference section for my talk is located at the end of this book. I find it interesting that the reference section for this talk is longer than the reference section for my dissertation (20 single-space pages vs. 13 single-space pages).

67 This link is still active.

68 There was a question-and-answer period after my talk that was not included in the video recording of my talk but was included in the audio recording. If one were to listen to the audio recording, the listener would note that those who were opposed to free speech engaged in emotional outbursts and personal attacks instead of asking me questions about the issues that I had raised in my talk.

was planning to make. In retrospect, I think that I was trying to be provocative in the sense of challenging much of the orthodoxy that is pervasive on university campuses these days, as opposed to being a provocateur who makes outrageous statements merely for the sake of doing so. I'll let the university community decide if I was successful in this endeavor.

There are three parts that I am hoping will spark the most discussion. The first was my argument that (at least in Canada) the attacks on free speech are coming from the left side of the political spectrum and that they're done using terminology from social justice (e.g., equity, inclusion, diversity). My main argument here was that what the terms imply and how they are used are sometimes very different from one another. As one example, I cited the recent black graduation ceremony that was held at the University of Toronto earlier this summer, which was enthusiastically endorsed by Kelly Hannah-Moffat, Vice President of Human Resources and Equity (slide 22 from my presentation). I cannot speak for others at this campus, but the thought of racial segregation terrifies me and suggests that we (as a society) are moving backwards instead of making progress.

The second part is the evidence I presented, which implies that conservative professors are justified in their fear of discrimination by their left/liberal colleagues (slides 47 and 48 from my presentation). I argued that this problem is likely arising because the political makeup of the professoriate has shifted markedly since the 1990s and that the liberal professors are asserting their power.

Related to my second point is my third one: With a lack of viewpoint diversity comes the problem of groupthink (large groups of people start to think the same way) and policies that are based on ideology instead of evidence. The particular example that I used was the mandatory equity (also known as diversity) workshops that are becoming increasingly commonplace in universities and many companies (slides 49 to 52 from my presentation), although I focused on our university in my talk. I argued that the first major problem with the workshops is that they equate equality of opportunity with equality of outcomes. Second, the only explanation that they consider is institutionalized bigotry in the form of racism, sexism, etc. Third, the evidence that is presented in the workshops is biased; in other words, the data that are presented are one-sided and not at all nuanced. Finally, I argued that the evidence for implicit bias and stereotype threat (the mechanisms that are used to explain the basis for the supposed institutionalized bigotry) is far too weak for these concepts to be applied in any fashion. I argued that the problems in these lines of research include: failure to replicate, publication bias, and small effect sizes. I believe that people will find the slide from an upcoming paper on stereotype threat to be interesting (slide 52). Based on this collective evidence, I argued that much more discussion, scrutiny, and review are warranted before any decisions can be made that involve implementing or continuing to implement these types of equity initiatives at this campus.

The feedback that I got on my suggestions for potential solutions (slides 70 and 71) on the issue of free speech was encouraging. Given that the university is looking to revise its strategic plan, I am hoping that the recommendations that I have made will spark discussion and that my suggestions can contribute to a strategic plan that strengthens the academic mission of our institution.

Sincerely,
Rick

October 19, 2017

On October 19, 2017, I uploaded a video recording of my talk onto my YouTube channel. Because I wanted to get feedback about my talk from people outside of Acadia University before making an announcement within the university community, one of the people I reached out to was Matthew Foldi (the face of Students for Free Expression). Below is a copy of the email message that I sent him at 1:43 p.m. that day:

Hi Matthew,

Here's the video link for the talk I gave on free speech: https://youtu.be/u73kjWyRRWU. I'd love to get your feedback (assuming you can get the time to listen/watch the talk) and would be honoured if you thought it was worth sharing on the Students for Free Expression Facebook page.

Thanks so much,
Rick

October 23, 2017

At 4:05 p.m. on October 23, 2017, I received the following enthusiast response from Mr. Foldi:

Professor Mehta,

I just had a chance to watch the entire talk and it was absolutely fabulous and distilled the issue so effectively into core ways of relating to everyone from scientists to activists to feminists, and beyond.

Thank you SO much for sending this to me. I just shared it on our page :)

Matthew

When I checked the Students for Free Expression's Facebook page, I noticed that Matthew posted the following comment: "Professor Rick Mehta at Acadia University in Canada gave one of the best articulations of free expression that we've seen in a long time. Watch here: https://youtu.be/u73kjWyRRWU"

Given that I do not expect the reader to take me at my word, below is a screenshot of the Students for Free Expression's post:

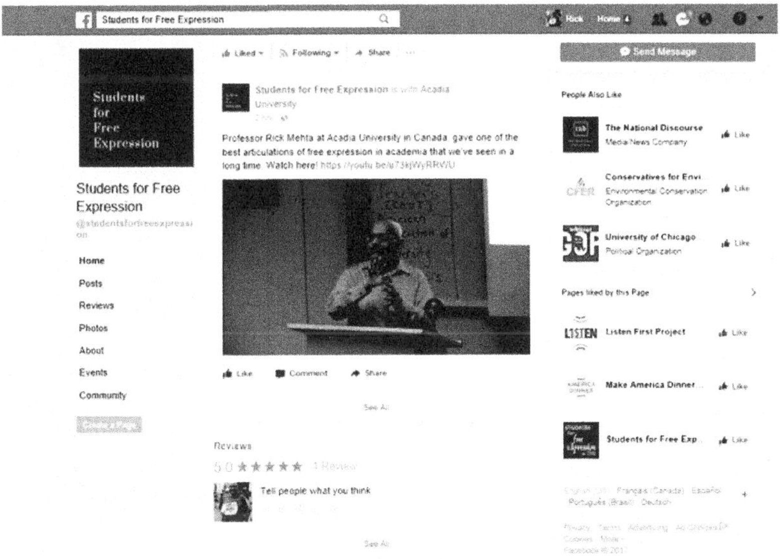

Because I was excited about the feedback that I had received from Mr. Foldi, I reached out to Dr. Barb Anderson (Designated Head for Rick Mehta; also a member of the Women in Science and Engineering [WISE] group at Acadia) by sending her an email message at 7:15 p.m. with the subject heading "Initial External Feedback on My Talk on Free Speech." Below is a copy of that message:

Hi Barb,

I'm forwarding you the email message I received from Matthew Foldi, who is the main organizer of a student group in the US called "Students for Free Expression." As well, I have attached a screenshot of what he posted on the group's Facebook page. While the initial feedback that I've been receiving from my talk has been quite positive, only time will tell if it will go viral on the internet.

Regarding the email I sent to the Faculty and Staff list earlier today [I will get to this issue later in this section of the book], I'd like to meet with you next week on how to strategize so that I can get the relevant bodies of faculty and administration to listen to what I have to say. My impression at this stage is that I have a lot of students behind me. After the talk, some of them approached me and said that they were initially uncomfortable about the issue of free speech but that I had won them over. The gist of the other comments I have received is that the conservative students felt that someone had spoken up for them, while the liberal students didn't feel the least bit threatened by what I had to say. The main opposition I'm getting is from faculty, as evidenced by the questions that I received at my talk.

There's no need for you to respond to this message tonight. We can talk further when I see you tomorrow morning.

Take care,
Rick

When I saw Dr. Anderson the next day, I noticed that she appeared to be visibly uncomfortable. When I asked her about meeting with me, she stated that she was really busy and walked away. At the time, I was perplexed and thought to myself, "I wonder what that was all about." I hope that the remainder of this section will answer that question.

At 10:11 a.m. on October 23, 2017, I sent an email message to the faculty and staff at Acadia University in which I informed everyone that my talk had been posted on my YouTube channel and in which I warned against ignoring the importance of free speech. Below is a copy of the message that I sent:

Good Morning Acadia Community,

I finally had a chance to post the talk that I gave on free speech on Wednesday, September 27 titled "Free Speech in Universities: Threats and Opportunities" on YouTube. Here is the link: https://youtu.be/u73kjWyRRWU

Given that the university is about to embark on reviewing its strategic plan, I am requesting that the university community consider this talk as a formal submission to this process. With regard to content, this talk reviews threats to free speech that are pervasive in the university system – with the incident at Evergreen State College this past summer being a cautionary tale for the direction in which Acadia is heading. As well, it includes a call to action and lays the groundwork for ways that universities can address the issue of free speech, which is a key requirement for academic freedom. However, the ultimate and overarching goal of this talk is to bridge the political divides in a world that is getting increasingly polarized, with universities taking the lead on this front.

I am hoping that the ideas that I have in this talk will be discussed seriously at the Senate and any other relevant governing body on campus, and will be working on doing what I can to ensure that this document makes its way to the relevant committees. As I had mentioned in an email I sent out prior to the talk, I wanted the Acadia community to have all the information needed so that they can rigorously scrutinize all of the ideas that I presented. To facilitate this process, I have made the slides and the sources that I read/reviewed to put the talk together accessible from the page on which my talk is posted. The list of sources is 20 pages long, and would have been longer had I used a format such as MLA or APA.

I don't think this topic is one that can be ignored and I would argue that it is one that is of interest and relevance to students. According to the official statistics that I received from The Athenaeum, there were 46 to 50 people in attendance at the talk and 256 people who listened to the talk on Axe Radio (the vast majority of people in attendance at my talk were students, and I am assuming that the demographics were similar for the listeners of Axe Radio). In other words, this is the equivalent of filling up Huggins 10 [the largest classroom at Acadia University] on a weeknight when classes are being held.

I will end this message by thanking The Athenaeum for hosting my talk, the Acadia Student Union for endorsing it, and Axe Radio for livestreaming it. Finally, I am grateful to Terry Aulenbach for recording and putting together this video.

Sincerely,
Rick

It did not take long until I started receiving opposition. At 10:40 a.m., Dr. Cynthia Bruce (a colleague from the School of Education; she went on to become President of the Acadia University Faculty Association in April 2019) sent me an email message in which she stated that my views were "disturbing" and in which she accused me of "advocating for oppression," "silencing marginalized voices," and "advancing human rights violations." At the time, I found it odd that she had copied the Dean of Science (Dr. Jeff Hooper) and one of my colleagues from my department (Dr. Randy Lynn Newman), who plays a prominent role with the women's groups at Acadia's campus, on this message.

After I present her email message to you (the reader), I will tell you a little bit about Dr. Bruce and the significance of the people who were copied on her response to me. Below is a copy of the email message that she sent me:

Dear Rick,

I appreciate you telling us that you will be making this a formal submission to the strategic planning committee. Rest assured I will make a counter-submission that will aim to work against the claims you have made – assertions that are largely substantiated by newspaper and opinion pieces. While I certainly acknowledge your right to speak, I find your anti-equity and anti-social justice stance truly disturbing. It is antithetical to the mission of our institution, and it comes dangerously close to advocating oppression. It is becoming increasingly clear to me that your aim is not to generate discussion about this critical topic. As I analyze your talk and the emails you send to the community, I have little choice but to conclude that you are working to silence marginalized voices; and specifically those voices, like mine, that have to fight daily to

claim our rightful places in institutions of higher learning.
Rick, as I indicated in a previous email, I will fight every day for equity and diversity. There is no place in institutions that clam to be open and progressive for the kinds of human rights violations that you advance when you call for universities to abandon social justice. So I will certainly ensure my submission includes the increasing body of research that provides evidence to post-secondary institutions around existing inequities and forward-thinking solutions.

Regards,

Cynthia

While Dr. Bruce's email message to me gives the reader glimpses into the contents of her character, her profile on Twitter provides other information that is more revealing. Her Twitter handle is "@blindacademic" and her profile description starts with "blind activist academic." The fact that she makes multiple references to being blind demonstrates that she is obsessed with her disability, i.e., that it forms a core part of her identity. And the fact that she uses the word "activist" before the word "academic" in her profile description demonstrates that she is an activist who happens to be an academic. I raise this issue because, during the semester in which Dr. Bruce emailed me, I told my students that I am an academic who happens to be a union member whereas my colleagues are union members who happen to be academics.

In my talk, I stated that one of the problems of our time has to do with the approaches that activists use to fight perceived or real injustices. At the time, I was not familiar with the works of Thomas Sowell or what he had to say about activists: "Activism is a way for useless people to feel important, even if the consequences of their activism are counterproductive for those they claim to be helping and damaging to the fabric of society as a whole."

I will now disclose the significance of Dr. Bruce having copied the Dean of Science (Dr. Jeff Hooper) and Dr. Randy Lynn Newman[69] (Department

69 Interestingly, Dr. Newman's Twitter handle is "@Neuro_WISE." If people do not use their names as their Twitter handle, they will often use the characteristics about themselves that speak to their identity or sense of self. In Dr. Newman's case, she was hired to teach courses on the biological foundations of behaviour, which explains the "Neuro" part of her handle. During her time at Acadia, Dr. Newman became involved with the women's groups on campus, so much so that they became (if they were not already) a core part of her identity or sense of self, which explains why the second part of her Twitter handle is "WISE."

of Psychology;[70] current Head of the Department)—who is active with the women's groups on campus—on her email message to me. It turns out that her act of copying the Dean on her email message to me was how she submitted a formal complaint against me; a key point to remember is that activists interpret disagreement as "harassment" or "intimidation." As for the significance of Dr. Bruce copying Dr. Newman on this message, it took me a few years until I could prove it, but Dr. Bruce's action revealed that Dr. Newman has skeletons in her closet. When I later took Acadia University and the Acadia University Faculty Association to court, my union submitted an affidavit to the Supreme Court of Nova Scotia on December 13, 2021, that included much of the "confidential" information that was in Acadia University's possession that the university and my union used to justify my dismissal.[71] While I was reviewing the collection of rumours and innuendo that was used as "evidence" against me, I saw a sentence written by Dr. Newman that caught my eye and is a smoking gun that proves my innocence: "He spent the last 45 minutes of his talk on free speech bashing WISE [Women in Science and Engineering] and the Union."

I hope that it is now clear to the reader that by the time that the *Chronicle Herald* published its article with the front page headline "Professor Defends Beyak's Remarks," my colleagues and the administration at Acadia University were strongly motivated to not only have me removed from the institution, but to also ruin my reputation so that I would be viewed as a pariah within my local community and within society at large. This explains why the university never gave me the severance pay that they are required to give their employees when they terminate their livelihoods without cause, i.e., in the absence of professional misconduct. For context, I will note that non-unionized employees who are terminated without cause typically receive 1 month of pay for each year that they worked plus damages. In other words, had I been fired without cause from a job in the private sector, I would have been entitled to receive 15 months

70 As an aside, I will mention that on August 2, 2017, I received an email message from Dr. Diane Holmberg in which she concluded with the following sentence: "Please stop before you damage reputations further, not least your own." I found it interesting that she asked me to "stop damaging reputations," given that I had not named anyone in any of the email messages that I circulated to the Acadia University community. I am adding this comment because I eventually came to realize that the goal of my colleagues and of the administration was to not only dismiss me from Acadia University but to also damage my reputation. I am fine with the university having terminated my employment because that is their prerogative. However, I am not fine with having my reputation ruined when I did nothing wrong, and to-my-dying-day I will fight for my family's honour.

71 I was shocked when I received these documents. From what I can tell, my union included these documents because they thought that they would disparage me in a court of law. Justice Smith should have ruled the affidavit inadmissible because it included anonymous information. The fact that she treated the defendants as credible when they were clearly lying in a court of law speaks to the corruption in Canada's legal system.

of pay plus damages. Instead, the university reneged on the deal that we reached when we settled the employment dispute on April 1, 2019, and then paid an arbitrator to rule that my employment was terminated "for cause," when all they had to do was pay the arbitrator to rule that I broke the first two rules of severance pay and therefore was no longer entitled to receive severance pay.[72]

My professional opinion in my capacity as a cognitive psychologist is that the conduct of Dr. Newman and my other opponents at Acadia University is eerily consistent with that of Dr. Robert Hare's description of how psychopaths conduct themselves (e.g., *Without Conscience: The Disturbing World of the Psychopaths Among Us* (1999)). Unfortunately, most people think of Canadian universities as being institutions that have been put into place to serve the public's interests when in fact they are Crown corporations, i.e., private companies that are owned by the Royal Family (hence the reference to a "crown"), that are expected to serve the Royal Family's interests even though they are funded with the Canadian taxpayer's money. For those who are interested, Dr. Hare's work has been cited in high-profile and eye-opening documentaries such as *The Corporation* (2003; Zeitgeist Films); I highly recommend that readers watch this documentary if they have not already seen it.[73]

Another piece of the puzzle is that corporations offer people opportunities to attain wealth and power. In addition, unionized workforces are designed to reward people who are lazy and/or incompetent. Given that Canadian universities are unionized corporations that are masquerading as institutions of higher learning, it should be no surprise that they are interested in recruiting and retaining people who lack a conscience. One variable that is unique to Acadia University is that it is a corporation that is based in a rural part of the country and therefore attracts professors and administrators who want to be a big fish in a small pond, which explains why the institution is run by narcissists and by fools who see themselves as wise.

72 This comment will make a lot more sense to fans of the book or movie *Fight Club*, which is about underground fighting clubs that are run by disaffected men.

73 More recently, a sequel titled "*The New Corporation: The Unfortunately Necessary Sequel*" was released. I am not commenting on this documentary because I have not seen it yet.

October 26, 2017

At this stage, it should be clear to the reader that I had support from the students who had seen my talk but that I was being opposed by the administration and my union. It should also be clear that the administration and/or my union had influenced Mr. Kondapuram (editor-in-chief, The Athenaeum), who would later submit complaints against me and encourage others to do so as well. The last piece of the puzzle is proving to the public that my colleagues also influenced Ms. Hamilton-Burge (President of the Acadia Students' Union), who would also go on to submit complaints against me and encourage others to do so.

At 4:14 p.m. on October 26, 2017, Ms. Hamilton-Burge sent me an email message with the subject heading "Language Clarification," which I thought was an odd heading. In her message, she claimed that the student union had not "endorsed" my talk, even though they had:

Hello Dr. Mehta,

I clarified with Sid earlier in the week around the freedom of speech talk that was given earlier in the year and wanted to clarify the language with you as well so we can be on the same page. We supported the event taking place as it was an Ath even but the word endorse is never used with any event because that's not our practice. We acknowledge and respect your opinion and talk, but we do not specifically endorse your talk. We supported the Ath in having their freedom of speech event.

I hope this clarifies language moving forward!

Thanks,
Grace

Because I had used the word "endorse" when I thanked the student union in the email message that I sent to Acadia's faculty and staff and had used the word "support" when I posted my video on my YouTube channel, I was perplexed by Ms. Hamilton-Burge's mincing of words. The only way that she could have known that I had used the word "endorse" was if a colleague had forwarded my email message to her. To confirm my suspicion, I informed Ms. Hamilton-Burge that I had used the word "support" when I posted the video on my YouTube channel. As I had expected, she responded by disclosing that I had used the word "endorse" in the email message that I had sent to Acadia's faculty and staff. Below is my response to Ms. Hamilton-Burge, which I sent at 4:23 p.m. on October 26, 2017:

Hi Grace,

I checked my YouTube page to find the exact wording that I used, and it is as follows:

"This talk was hosted by The Athenaeum (Acadia's student-run independent newspaper; theath.ca), supported by the Acadia Student Union (theasu.ca), and livestreamed by Axe Radio (axeradio.ca). I am also grateful to Terry Aulenbach for recording and putting together this video."

If there is another context in which my actions led to this miscommunication, please let me know so that I can rectify it right away. I take the working relationship that I have with the ASU very seriously and would not do anything to jeopardize this relationship.

Thank you,
Rick

And below is the response that I received from her at 4:28 p.m.:

Hello Dr. Mehta,

Thank you for the prompt reply! I believe the endorsement word was used in an email that was sent out to staff and faculty. Just moving forward if we can use the word support that'd be good.

Thanks!
Grace

I clearly caught Ms. Hamilton-Burge in a lie.

Given that I have proven that the administration at Acadia University, the faculty association at Acadia University, the people running the student-run newspaper at Acadia University, and the executive of the student union at Acadia University are liars, then the only conclusion that can be derived is that Acadia University terminated my employment as a tenured professor because I defended the truth and the values that go with it: honesty and transparency.

Epilogue: Bizumic et al. (2017) Revisited

Am I ready for the real world?
Will I pass the test?
You know it's a jungle out there
Ain't nothin' gonna stop me, I won't be second best
But the joke's on those who believe the system's fair

—Bryan Adams/Jim Vallance, "Teacher Teacher"

When I delivered my talk on September 27, 2017, I did not take into consideration the fact that Bizumic et al. (2017) were biased in their approach to their research. For this reason, I am revisiting this paper.

The question that motivated the research in this paper was: Has tolerance for diversity in cultural backgrounds led to intolerance for opposing viewpoints? A problem with this question is that it assumes that all cultural backgrounds are based on similar values and are therefore compatible with each other. However, Sir John Glubb's (1976; *The Fate of Empires and Search for Survival*) analysis of the themes that emerge in the history of humanity reveals that societies fall when they allow for immigration, especially when the immigrants do not share the same values as the country that has adopted them as citizens.

Thus, the only people who would tolerate "diversity" in cultural backgrounds are people who are opposed to the country in which they live and therefore want to see their country fail. This is the only reason why people would agree with an objectively false statement such as "The values, ways of life, and customs of other cultures are probably just as good as my own." A person who agrees with this statement would condone immoral and barbaric practices such as female genital mutilation on the basis of "tolerance."

From a moral standpoint, a more accurate way of wording the question of interest in Bizumic et al.'s (2017) paper is: Is tolerance for immorality or a lie associated with an intolerance for morality or the truth? We get a different interpretation of the results of Study 1b when the findings are analyzed through this lens. In the case of Study 1b, participants completed a measure of "ethnic tolerance" and were asked if they would accept or reject a person based on the extent to which they agreed or disagreed that "asylum seekers" ("economic migrants" is a more accurate term) should be detained. The authors found that people who scored high on the measure of "ethnic tolerance" were opposed to detaining people who entered their country illegally and would reject people who thought that it was a good idea to screen people who wish to immigrate to their country to ensure that they are doing it through the proper channels. In contrast, the authors found that people who scored low on their measure of "ethnic tolerance" were in favour of detaining people who entered their country illegally but would not reject people based on the position they took on the issue of detaining "asylum seekers." Worded somewhat differently, the results of this study suggest that people who are immoral insist on other people also being immoral, while people who have morals have little interest in imposing their morality on others.

An alternative and perhaps more accurate interpretation of their analysis of Study 4 is that people whose identities are based on lies are highly likely to reject people who have beliefs that are based on truth because people who have beliefs based on lies do not identify with people who have beliefs based on truth. In contrast, people who have beliefs that are based on truth are not going to discriminate against others based on their beliefs, i.e., advocates for truth support people's right to be wrong. The most plausible explanation is that the truth does not mind being questioned, whereas a lie hates being challenged.

And this, ladies and gentlemen, gets at the heart of the problems of today.

So the years go on and on, but nothing's lost or won
And what you learned is soon forgotten
They take the best years of your life
Try to tell you wrong from right
But you walk away with nothing

—Bryan Adams/Jim Vallance, "Teacher Teacher"

Sources Used for My Talk ("Free Speech in Universities: Threats and Opportunities")

Addo, Koran

Instructor at Harris-Stowe gets almost $5 million in racial discrimination suit: http://www.stltoday.com/news/local/crime-and-courts/instructor-at-harris-stowe-gets-almost-million-in-racial-discrimination/article_a72e6120-e535-597b-b5e8-dedaa64386bf.html

Agarwall, Rajshree

Afraid to speak up: In the era of trigger warnings, a tenured professor stays silent: https://www.washingtonpost.com/news/grade-point/wp/2016/10/04/afraid-to-speak-up-in-the-era-of-trigger-warnings-a-tenured-professor-stays-silent/?utm_term=.9f09b629be84

Air Passenger Rights

Air Passenger Bill: Opening statement by Dr. Gabor Lukacs to the House of Commons' TRAN Committee: https://www.youtube.com/watch?v=y95N7jFd0WY

Artuso, Antonella

Ryerson instructor tells student to only rely on feminist journals: http://www.torontosun.com/2017/03/09/ryerson-instructor-tells-student-to-only-rely-on-feminist-journals

Associated Press

Violent protest prompts Berkely to cancel talk by Breitbart editor: http://www.cbc.ca/news/world/berkeley-milo-yiannopoulos-protest-1.3963052

Auburn Reporter

Fortunato bill aims to end state support for Evergreen State College: https://archive.is/x5Zcb

Badger Pundit YouTube Page

This page contains footage from a) the Law & Justice Work Session that took place at the Washington State Senate, and b) the meeting of Evergreen State College's Board of Trustees in the aftermath of the events that transpired at the college. Below are some noteworthy clips (I cringe at the title of the first one, though):

Evergreen President: We've made a mess of things. So give us MORE money! Social justice!: https://www.youtube.com/watch?v=yAFmnfXivfk

Evergreen State College, Board of Trustees meeting, 7/12/2017 [contains the entire meeting]: https://www.youtube.com/watch?v=yL54iN8dxuo

Prof. Matt Wanweller: Leftist college students see language and violence as the same thing: https://www.youtube.com/watch?v=SpYx38KjlFA

Prof. Michael Paros: Evergreen needs to teach students HOW to think, not WHAT to think: https://www.youtube.com/watch?v=yNNxX-ptUow

Balan, Matthew

Chaos at college in Washington state as leftists roam campus with bats, assault trolling chalker: https://www.mediaite.com/online/chaos-at-college-in-washington-state-as-leftists-roam-campus-with-bats-assault-trolling-chalker/

Barrett, Lisa Feldman

When is speech violence?: https://www.nytimes.com/2017/07/14/opinion/sunday/when-is-speech-violence.html?_r=0

Bartlett, Tom

Can we really measure implicit bias? Maybe not: http://www.chronicle.com/article/Can-We-Really-Measure-Implicit/238807?cid=at&utm_source=at&utm_medium=en&elqTrackId=6c65e0853c3f4d82befeb09f3b704aa0&elq=e02fa393fe484aaa8833c2b7e79633eb&elqaid=12009&elqat=1&elqCampaignId=4836

BBC News

Cardiff Metropolitan Uni bans 'gender stereotype' words: http://www.bbc.com/news/uk-wales-south-east-wales-39153731

Beatty, Dave

McMaster debate with controversial professor Jordan Peterson disrupted by activists: http://www.cbc.ca/news/canada/hamilton/mcmaster-debate-with-controversial-professor-jordan-peterson-disrupted-by-activists-1.4031843

Beeby, Dean

Revenue Canada targets bird watchers for political activity: http://www.cbc.ca/news/politics/revenue-canada-targets-birdwatchers-for-political-activity-1.2799546

Belluck, Pam

Brown U. to examine debt to slave trade: http://www.nytimes.com/2004/03/13/us/brown-u-to-examine-debt-to-slave-trade.html?mcubz=3

Best-Raiten, Ashley

In Lower Merion, Democrats and Republicans try something new: Listening to each other: http://www.philly.com/philly/opinion/commentary/lower-merion-trump-charlottesville-republicans-democrats-hate-love-election-20170828.html

Bilello, Joe

College reinstates professor who said to let White people "f-ing die": https://www.mediaite.com/print/college-reinstates-professor-who-said-to-let-white-people-fing-die/

Bizumic, Boris and colleagues

Bizumic, B., Kenny, A., Iyer, R., Tanuwira, J., & Huxley, E. (2017). Are the ethnically tolerant free of discrimination, prejudice, and political intolerance? *European Journal of Social Psychology*. doi: 10.1002/ejsp.2263

Blankmanship, Donna Gordon

Protest, but not violence, is part of the DNA of this nation and the Evergreen State College: http://www.seattletimes.com/opinion/protest-but-not-violence-is-part-of-the-dna-of-this-nation-and-the-evergreen-state-college/

Blatchford, Christie

"An opportunity to make their displeasure known": Pronoun professor denied government grant: http://nationalpost.com/news/canada/an-opportunity-to-make-their-displeasure-known-government-pulls-funding-of-pronoun-professor

If gender identity debate at U of T was about free speech, then the battle is truly lost: http://nationalpost.com/opinion/christie-blatchford-if-gender-identity-debate-at-u-of-t-was-about-free-speech-then-the-battle-is-truly-lost

Proud boys behaviour might be goofy, but is hardly 'deplorable': http://nationalpost.com/opinion/christie-blatchford-proud-boys-behaviour-might-be-goofy-but-hardly-deplorable

Truth is, universities have never been champions of free speech: http://nationalpost.com/opinion/christie-blatchford-truth-is-universities-have-never-been-champions-of-free-speech

Boucher, Joanne

Dress code message at U of W sexist: https://www.winnipegfreepress.com/opinion/analysis/dress-code-message--at-u-of-w-sexist-307799831.html

Free speech a crucial part of university's purpose: https://www.winnipegfreepress.com/opinion/analysis/free-speech-a-crucial-part-of-universitys-purpose-446318333.html#have-your-say

Boyce, Benjamin A. [YouTube Channel]

URL for his channel: https://www.youtube.com/channel/UCm13xHVNFVwzHzK3QHSaZ3Q/feed

Benjamin Boyce is a former poet who now works primarily as a critic of postmodernism's intrusion into US education. He had little activity on his YouTube page until the events at Evergreen State College. Since then, he has been investigating the events that led to the carnage that unfolded earlier this year. Through the use of freedom of information, he has tracked down informative email exchanges. He has also tracked down video footage of the information given out in the sessions that fell under the themes of diversity, equity, inclusion, systemic racism, etc. I've posted the links for the videos that I have watched thus far; he has made 14 other relevant videos that I have not yet checked out. My impression of Benjamin is that he articulates himself clearly and that most of his analyses are spot on. The videos that I have watched thus far are listed in alphabetical order.

Anti-"whiteness" at Evergreen State College: https://www.youtube.com/watch?v=xRCdUsJRxoM

At Evergreen, supremacy is the new privilege: https://www.youtube.com/watch?v=3_2_gpDXvUI

Biased training at Evergreen: https://www.youtube.com/watch?v=gr8MCxW_PLw

Dumbing data down at Evergreen: https://www.youtube.com/watch?v=qTVl5OwnvU4

Evergreen's devolutionary: https://www.youtube.com/watch?v=VgERJbT4JQM

'Hide your maces and tasers' – Bret Weinstein's student speaks about protests: https://www.youtube.com/watch?v=h5vPKwlIbCE

Is Evergreen a cult?: https://www.youtube.com/watch?v=VfVRaExw1lI

Multicultural Mans(i)on family at Evergreen: https://www.youtube.com/watch?v=wJLio0TCwKc

Social justice at Evergreen: https://www.youtube.com/watch?v=Jye2C5r-QA0

Stunted by social justice: An Evergreen student [McKenzie Kyger] speaks: https://www.youtube.com/watch?v=6uTm7_GE6So

The red queen of Evergreen: https://www.youtube.com/watch?v=ucJgYsylSOY

The underlying causes of Evergreen unrest: https://www.youtube.com/watch?v=bafjepm_EYo
Unlearning Evergreen: https://www.youtube.com/watch?v=QYs5f1lpkOA

Brehm, Christina

Does banning hate speech eliminate hatred? The case of East Germany (talk given at the Annual General Meeting of the Society for Academic Freedom and Scholarship): https://www.youtube.com/watch?v=I1OcBk3N27s&feature=youtu.be

Bridges, George S.

Why students need trigger warnings and safe places: http://www.seattletimes.com/opinion/why-students-need-trigger-warnings-and-safe-places/

Brooks, Arthur C.

Don't shun conservative professors: https://www.nytimes.com/2017/09/15/opinion/conservative-professors.html?emc=eta1&_r=1

Bruni, Frank

These campus inquisitions must stop: https://www.nytimes.com/2017/06/03/opinion/sunday/bruni-campus-inquisitions-evergreen-state.html?mcubz=3

Bueckert, Kate

Wilfred Laurier University Grad Student Association blasted for terminating café operator over help wanted ad: http://www.cbc.ca/news/canada/kitchener-waterloo/wilfrid-laurier-university-gsa-cafe-veritas-contract-1.3900665

Buncombe, Andrew

Ivy league university funded by slave trader confronts its past: http://www.independent.co.uk/news/world/americas/ivy-league-university-funded-by-slave-trader-confronts-its-past-566493.html

Canadian Press

Is Lou Reed's 'Walk on the Wild Side' transphobic? Guelph student union apologizes for playing song: http://nationalpost.com/news/canada/is-lou-reeds-walk-on-the-wild-side-transphobic-guelph-student-union-apologizes-for-playing-song

Card, Jean

It's not too late for Free Speech: https://www.usnews.com/opinion/thomas-jefferson-street/articles/2017-09-22/facebook-can-help-college-students-learn-about-free-speech?src=usn_fb

CBC Radio Day 6 with David Bambury

Indigenous children are dying while Ottawa fights a ruling that calls for action: http://www.cbc.ca/radio/day6/episode-347-cindy-blackstock-seeks-justice-man-vs-beast-steve-jobs-opera-women-s-rights-in-saudi-and-more-1.4213358/indigenous-children-are-dying-while-ottawa-fights-a-ruling-that-calls-for-action-1.4213378

Chason, Rachel

A black blues musician has a unique hobby: Befriending white supremacists: https://www.washingtonpost.com/news/morning-mix/wp/2017/08/30/a-black-blues-musician-has-an-unique-hobby-befriending-white-supremacists/?utm_term=.c839c9703a1d

Csananady, Ashley

Men's issues group taking Ryerson University's student union to court over club status: http://nationalpost.com/news/canada/mens-issues-group-taking-ryerson-universitys-student-union-to-court-over-club-status

Deane, Patrick

Academic freedom and the role of the academy: An open letter to the McMaster community: http://dailynews.mcmaster.ca/article/academic-freedom-and-the-role-of-the-academy-an-open-letter-to-the-mcmaster-community/

Dershowitz, Alan M.

Both the left and the right must guard against campus extremism: https://www.bostonglobe.com/opinion/2017/08/31/both-left-and-right-must-guard-against-campus-extremism/7xL7NYfpD2r0EELDHf6c0L/story.html?event=event25#comments

DiManno, Rosie

Marie Henein-haters part of a worrying trend: https://www.thestar.com/news/gta/2016/11/24/marie-henein-haters-part-of-a-worrying-trend-dimanno.html

Dobbin, Frank & Kalev, Alexandra

Why diversity programs fail: https://hbr.org/2016/07/why-diversity-programs-fail

Dormon, Peter

The protests at Evergreen State College, Un-Foxed: http://econospeak.blogspot.ca/2017/05/the-protests-at-evergreen-state-college.html

Economist (February 15, 2017)
Article on Young People and Free Speech: https://www.economist.com/blogs/graphicdetail/2017/02/daily-chart-10?fsrc=scn/fb/te/bl/ed/youngpeopleandfreespeech

Economist (September 7, 2017)
Arguments over free speech on campus are not left v right: https://www.economist.com/news/united-states/21728688-reed-college-oregon-shows-left-v-left-clashes-can-be-equally-vitriolic-arguments

Elections Nova Scotia
Official Results of General Election (May 30, 2017): http://results.electionsnovascotia.ca/Summary.aspx

Ernt, Douglas
Trinity College professor's anti-white 'f-ing die' scandal cost school $200K in lost donations [Johnny Eric Williams]: http://www.washingtontimes.com/news/2017/aug/2/trinity-college-johnny-eric-williams-anti-white-f-/

Factual Feminist [YouTube posts by Christina Hoff Sommers that are hosted by the American Enterprise Institute]
Do men need to check their privilege?: https://www.youtube.com/watch?v=cRsYwu8uD4I
The gender wage gap uses bogus statistics: https://www.youtube.com/watch?v=58arQIr882w

Flaherty, Coleen
Trinity Suspends Targeted Professor [Johnny Eric Williams, Trinity College]: https://www.insidehighered.com/news/2017/06/27/trinity-college-connecticut-puts-johnny-eric-williams-leave-over-controversial

Fleishman, Jeffrey
A black man's quixotic quest to quell the racism of the KKK, one robe at a time: http://www.latimes.com/entertainment/movies/la-ca-film-accidental-courtesy-20161205-story.html

Freethink
How can the left and right understand each other? By sitting down for dinner: https://www.circa.com/story/2017/07/17/politics/make-american-dinner-again-helps-democrats-republicans-understand-each-other

Friedersdorf, Conor

The audacity of talking about race with the Klu Klux Klan: https://www.theatlantic.com/politics/archive/2015/03/the-audacity-of-talking-about-race-with-the-klu-klux-klan/388733/

The most shortsighted attack on free speech in modern U.S. history: https://www.theatlantic.com/amp/article/537468/

Furey, Anthony

Political correctness used to be a joke, now it's downright scary: http://www.torontosun.com/2017/05/20/political-correctness-used-to-be-a-joke-now-its-downright-scary

Gatehouse, Jonathon

When science goes silent: http://www.macleans.ca/news/canada/when-science-goes-silent/

Gee, Marcus

Speakers' corner: Where all speech reigns free: https://beta.theglobeandmail.com/news/world/speakers-corner-where-all-speech-reigns-free/article36364266/?ref=http://www.theglobeandmail.com

Gersen, Jeannie Suk

Laura Kipniss's endless trial by Title IX: https://www.newyorker.com/news/news-desk/laura-kipniss-endless-trial-by-title-ix

Gilley, Bruce

Why I'm leaving the Political Science Association: http://www.mindingthecampus.org/2017/08/why-im-leaving-the-political-science-association/?utm_content=buffer961cd&utm_medium=social&utm_source=twitter.com&utm_campaign=buffer

Gordon, Andrea

University of Toronto gets ready for first-ever Black graduation ceremony: https://www.thestar.com/yourtoronto/education/2017/06/19/university-of-toronto-gets-ready-for-first-ever-black-graduation-ceremony.html

Haag, Matthew

Chelsea Manning's Harvard Fellowship withdrawn after criticism: https://www.nytimes.com/2017/09/14/us/chelsea-manning-harvard-fellow-cia.html

Haidt, Jonathan

The site "Righteous Mind" contains a variety of articles that Jonathan Haidt and others have written on viewpoint diversity in the academy, as well as links to his talks that are commonly known as "Truth University vs Social Justice University" and "Coddling University vs. Strengthening University": http://righteousmind.com/viewpoint-diversity/

Intimidation is the new normal on campus: http://www.chronicle.com/article/Intimidation-Is-the-New-Normal/239890

Professors must now fear intimidation from both sides: https://heterodoxacademy.org/2017/06/28/professors-must-now-fear-intimidation-from-both-sides/

The amazing 1969 prophecy that racial preferences would cause the exact grievances of protestors today: https://heterodoxacademy.org/2016/05/12/the-amazing-1969-prophecy/

The blasphemy case against Bret Weinstein, and its four lessons for professors: https://heterodoxacademy.org/2017/05/27/this-weeks-witch-hunt/

Haidt, Jonathan & Lukianoff, Greg

Why it's a bad idea to tell students that words are violence: https://www.theatlantic.com/education/archive/2017/07/why-its-a-bad-idea-to-tell-students-words-are-violence/533970/

Hartocollis, Anemona

A campus argument goes viral. Now the college is under siege: https://www.nytimes.com/2017/06/16/us/evergreen-state-protests.html?mtrref=undefined&gwh=4EEFE7B6BE8BEBD1E9E81604C77F1EBC&gwt=pay

Haskell, David Millard

https://www.thestar.com/opinion/commentary/2017/03/16/free-speech-at-university-under-attack-again.html

Hauen, Jack

Facing pushback, Ryerson University cancels panel discussion on campus free speech: http://nationalpost.com/news/canada/facing-pushback-ryerson-cancels-panel-discussion-on-campus-free-speech

Hayward, Steven

Anarchy at Evergreen State: http://www.powerlineblog.com/archives/2017/06/anarchy-at-evergreen-state.php

Hoff Sommers, Christina

Wage gap myth exposed – By feminists: http://www.huffingtonpost.com/christina-hoff-sommers/wage-gap_b_2073804.html

Hutter, Kristy

Campus clash: Students battle over what constitutes free speech: http://www.cbc.ca/news/canada/free-speech-versus-hate-speech-1.4058994

Ibbitson, John

Your rights, my rights: Academic freedom faces off with a clarion call for safety on campus: https://beta.theglobeandmail.com/news/national/education/free-speech-university-campus/article35174756/?ref=http://www.theglobeandmail.com&

Illing, Sean

An Ivy League professor on what the campus conversation on race gets wrong: https://www.vox.com/platform/amp/2016/9/20/12915036/race-criminal-justice-inequality-glenn-loury-ta-nehisi-coates

Inbar, Yoel and Lammers, Joris

Inbar, Y., & Lammers, J. (2012). Political diversity in social and personality psychology. *Perspectives on Psychological Science, 7,* 496-503. doi: 10.1177/1745691618792

Independent Man [YouTube page]

This 20-minute video clip summarizes events at Evergreen State College. However, the commentary must be approached with caution because we know nothing about the person doing the voiceover. The footage from what took place is worth checking out, though.

Bret Weinstein & Evergreen State College: https://www.youtube.com/watch?v=ugBr6FnCKiY

Jacobson, William A.

Evergreen Prof. Bret Weinstein's greatest alleged sin? Not suffering in silence: http://legalinsurrection.com/2017/06/evergreen-prof-bret-weinsteins-greatest-alleged-sin-not-suffering-in-silence/

Justice Centre for Constitutional Freedoms

Release – Canadian Transportation Agency warned to cease censorship of air passengers rights advocate: https://www.jccf.ca/release-canadian-transportation-agency-warned-to-cease-censorship-of-air-passenger-rights-advocate/

Jussim, Lee

Is stereotype threat overcooked, overstated, and oversold?: https://heterodoxacademy.org/2015/12/30/is-stereotype-threat-overcooked-overstated-and-oversold/

Kabbany, Jennifer

Evergreen State College settles claim with embattled professors for $500,000: http://ussanews.com/News1/2017/09/15/evergreen-state-college-settles-claim-with-embattled-professors-for-500000/

Kane, Laura

Simon Fraser University professor launches petition to change 'The Clan' team name: https://www.thestar.com/sports/2017/09/22/simon-fraser-university-professor-launches-petition-to-change-the-clan-team-name.html

Kay, Barbara

Why does a report on 'gender equality' in mental health all but ignore the illnesses of men and boys?: http://nationalpost.com/opinion/barbara-kay-why-is-it-that-a-report-on-promoting-gender-equity-in-mental-health-all-but-ignores-the-illnesses-of-men-and-boys

Kipniss, Laura

Unwanted Advances: Sexual Paranoia Comes to Campus (book published in 2017)

Interview done with Steve Paiken on "The Agenda with Steve Paiken" called "Fear and Loathing in American Academia": https://www.youtube.com/watch?v=yihNgtJGpfk&t=22s

Interview with Reason TV – Laura Kipniss on how campus feminism infantilizes women: https://www.youtube.com/watch?v=6luo4U0joO0

Interview with Reason TV – Laura Kipness: How colleges criminalized sex: https://www.youtube.com/watch?v=Rg7ahG7N0Ns

Kristoff, Nicholas

A confession of liberal intolerance: https://www.nytimes.com/2016/05/08/opinion/sunday/a-confession-of-liberal-intolerance.html?_r=0

Lachance, Mike

Evergreen State leftist professor stunned as SJWs viciously turn on him: https://legalinsurrection.com/2017/05/evergreen-state-leftist-professor-stunned-as-sjws-viciously-turn-on-him/

Laucius, Joanne

After a 13-year battle, former Health Canada scientist won't get his job back: http://ottawacitizen.com/news/local-news/after-a-13-year-battle-former-health-canada-scientist-wont-get-his-job-back

Le, Natalie Bao Tram

I'm a female minority at Harvard, and I don't agree with PC culture: http://www.thecrimson.com/article/2017/6/13/dont-agree-pc-culture/#.WVxsthKFZZo.twitter

Leiter, Brian [Leiter Reports: A Philosophy Blog]

Implicit bias, stereotype threat, and the empirical literature: http://leiterreports.typepad.com/blog/2014/12/implicit-bias-stereotype.html

Lemoine, Phillipe

Why are women underrepresented in philosophy and should we care?: https://necpluribusimpar.net/women-underrepresented-philosophy-care/

Levy, Sue-Ann

University of Toronto's Black Graduation misses the mark: http://www.torontosun.com/2017/06/22/university-of-torontos-black-graduation-misses-the-mark

Lilienfeld, Scott O.

Lilienfeld, S.O. (2017). Microaggressions: Strong claims, inadequate evidence. *Perspectives on Psychological Science, 12,* 138-169. doi: 10.1177/1745691616659391

Lilla, Mark

The end of identity liberalism: https://www.nytimes.com/2016/11/20/opinion/sunday/the-end-of-identity-liberalism.html?_r=0

Long, Katherine

Long-simmering discord led to The Evergreen State College's viral moment: http://www.seattletimes.com/seattle-news/education/discord-at-evergreen-state-simmered-for-a-year-before-it-boiled-over/

Lott, Tim

Jordan Peterson and the transgender wars: https://life.spectator.co.uk/2017/09/jordan-peterson-and-the-transgender-wars/

Lukianoff, Greg & Haidt, Jonathan
The coddling of the American mind: https://www.theatlantic.com/magazine/archive/2015/09/the-coddling-of-the-american-mind/399356/

MacDonald, Neil
The budget's gender-based analysis forgot to look at one thing – men: https://www.nytimes.com/2016/11/20/opinion/sunday/the-end-of-identity-liberalism.html?_r=0

MacPherson, Paige
University students need to relax. It's just a hat: http://nationalpost.com/opinion/paige-macpherson-university-students-need-to-relax-its-just-a-hat

Makers (5 minute video on Ruth Simmons)
https://www.makers.com/ruth-simmons

Martin, Andrea
Gad Saad believes in free speech at (almost) all costs: http://www.theprovince.com/news/canada/saad+believes+free+speech+almost+costs/14695190/story.html?utm_source=dlvr.it&utm_medium=twitter

McFarland, Kelly
The Liberals over-promise and under-deliver on the Indigenous file: http://nationalpost.com/opinion/kelly-mcparland-the-liberals-over-promise-and-under-deliver-on-the-indigenous-file

McMaster University Presidential Advisory Committee on Building an Inclusive Community (PACBIC)
Statement re: McMaster event featuring Dr. Jordan Peterson (Professor of Psychology, University of Toronto): http://pacbic.mcmaster.ca/documents/FINALstatementreJordanPetersonevent_Mar162017.pdf

Melchior, Jillian Kay
Mizzou pays a price for appeasing the left: https://www.wsj.com/articles/mizzou-pays-a-price-for-appeasing-the-left-1503258538

Mikkelsen, Drew
Professor told he's not safe on campus after college protests: http://www.king5.com/news/local/olympia/professor-told-hes-not-safe-on-campus-after-college-protests/443098670

Miller, Geoffrey

The neurodiversity case for free speech: http://quillette.com/2017/07/18/neurodiversity-case-free-speech/

Monson, Doni

Rep. Matt Manweller aims to cut Evergreen off from state: https://mynorthwest.com/650230/manweller-evergreen-state-college-bill/

Montgomery, Marc

The new university "chill" tactic on free speech: http://www.rcinet.ca/en/2017/03/29/the-new-university-chill-tactic-on-free-speech/

Murphy, Rex

A whiff of BLM grapeshot, and Niki Ashton waves the surrender flag (I dare not call it 'white', in this context): http://nationalpost.com/opinion/rex-murphy-a-whiff-of-blm-grapeshot-and-niki-ashton-waves-the-surrender-flag-i-dare-not-call-it-white-in-this-context

'Antifa' are despicable fascists – call them that, openly, now: http://nationalpost.com/opinion/rex-murphy-antifa-are-despicable-fascists-call-them-that-openly-now

Celebrating 'diversity' will only divide us, but celebrating Canada' unity keeps us strong: http://nationalpost.com/opinion/rex-murphy-celebrating-diversity-will-only-divide-us-but-celebrating-canadas-unity-keeps-us-strong#comments-area

Deplorability of neo-Nazis no excuse for anti-fascist thuggery: http://nationalpost.com/opinion/rex-murphy-deplorability-of-neo-nazis-no-excuse-for-anti-fascist-thuggery

My name is Josephine [Josephine Mathias's YouTube page]

The reality is patriarchy: Indoctrination at Ryerson University: https://www.youtube.com/watch?v=6TcYlgAi7zQ

Neil, Aaron

Why it's time to stop worrying about First World 'Gender Gaps': http://quillette.com/2017/07/15/time-stop-worrying-first-world-gender-gaps/

Pells, Rachel

University bans phrases such as "mankind" and "gentleman's agreement" in favour of gender-neutral terms: http://www.independent.co.uk/student/news/university-cardiff-metropolitan-bans-phrases-mankind-gentlemans-agreement-gender-neutral-terms-free-a7609521.html

Peterson, Jordan B. (You Tube Page)

Debate on Bill C-16 and the Human Rights Code (also known as University of Toronto Free Speech Debate): https://www.youtube.com/watch?v=68NHUV5me7Q

Runnymede Society Queen's Debate: Professor Bruce Pardy (Queen's University), Professor Jordan Peterson (University of Toronto) [also known as Social Justice / Freedom of Speech: Bill C16 Debate Queen's Law School): https://www.youtube.com/watch?v=TAQlleqDgbI

Phillips, Kristine

Professor at criminal justice school called students 'future dead cops.' He's been suspended: http://nationalpost.com/news/world/a-professor-at-criminal-justice-called-students-future-dead-cops-hes-been-suspended

Professor Watchlist website

http://www.professorwatchlist.org/

Quilette Magazine

The Google Memo: Four scientists respond: http://quillette.com/2017/08/07/google-memo-four-scientists-respond/

Quintana, Chris

Trinity College of Conn. closes over threats after conservative website targets professor: http://www.chronicle.com/blogs/ticker/trinity-college-of-conn-closes-over-threats-after-conservative-website-targets-professor/119043

Rampall, Catherine

A chilling study shows how hostile college students are towards free speech: https://www.washingtonpost.com/opinions/a-chilling-study-shows-how-hostile-college-students-are-toward-free-speech/2017/09/18/cbb1a234-9ca8-11e7-9083-fbfddf6804c2_story.html?utm_term=.262849e0c790

Reilly, Katie

Evergreen State College resumes after violent threat and $10,000 in damage: http://time.com/4807225/evergreen-state-college-violence-vandalism-threat/

Richarz, Allan

The left and the right are in an all-out outrage arms race: http://www.cbc.ca/news/opinion/outrage-arms-race-1.4177480

Richardson, Bradford

College professor Bret Weinstein holds class off-campus, citing students threatening violence: http://www.washingtontimes.com/news/2017/may/27/bret-weinstein-evergreen-state-professor-holds-cla/

Routledge, Clay

Colleges are rejecting our common humanity and the science that reveals it: https://www.jamesgmartin.center/2017/04/colleges-rejecting-common-humanity-science-reveals/

Salzman, Philip Carl

Universities strive for diversity in everything but opinion: http://www.meforum.org/6366/no-diversity-of-opinion-on-campus

Welcome to the "Social Justice" University: https://www.gatestoneinstitute.org/9604/social-justice

Sampathkumar, Mythili

White professor was fired from predominantly black university due to colour of skin, court rules: http://www.independent.co.uk/news/world/americas/white-professor-was-fired-from-predominantly-black-university-due-to-colour-of-skin-court-rules-a7788171.html

Seattle Times Editorial Board

The Evergreen State College: No safety, no learning, no future: http://www.seattletimes.com/opinion/editorials/the-evergreen-state-college-no-safety-no-learning-no-future/

Seidgård, Cecilia Schelin

Sweden is not some kind of equality paradise: https://www.thelocal.se/20150310/sweden-is-not-some-kind-of-equality-paradise

Selley, Chris

Libraries feel the heat on freedom of speech: http://nationalpost.com/opinion/chris-selley-libraries-feel-the-heat-on-freedom-of-speech

Sesardic, Neven & De Clercq, R.

Women in Philosophy: Problems with the Discrimination Hypothesis: http://spot.colorado.edu/~tooley/Women%20in%20Philosophy-Problems%20with%20the%20Discrimination%20Hypothesis-National%20Association%20of%20Scholars.pdf

Sexton, John
Enrollment at Evergreen State College Drops 5%, Hiring Freeze to Follow: https://hotair.com/archives/2017/09/01/enrollment-evergreen-state-college-drops-5-hiring-freeze-follow/

Shimshock, Rob
'It's life or death for us: Students protest racism, police brutality at college: http://dailycaller.com/2017/05/25/its-life-or-death-for-us-students-protest-racism-police-brutality-at-college-video/

Singal, Jesse
Psychology's favorite tool for measuring racism isn't up to the job: http://nymag.com/scienceofus/2017/01/psychologys-racism-measuring-tool-isnt-up-to-the-job.html

Slavov, Sita
https://www.usnews.com/opinion/economic-intelligence/2014/05/29/college-students-dismiss-dialogue-when-protesting-commencement-speakers

Smith College (May 18, 2014; Ruth Simmons' commencement speech)
https://www.smith.edu/news/ruth-simmons-to-smith-college-graduates-ones-voice-grows-stronger-in-encounters-with-opposing-views/

Smith, Joanna
Trudeau government looks to limit debate on big priorities as Parliament returns: https://globalnews.ca/news/3750995/trudeau-government-debate-big-priorities-parliament-returns/

Smith, Marie-Danielle
NDP leadership candidate Ashton defends deleting Beyoncé meme after accusations of cultural appropriation: http://nationalpost.com/news/politics/niki-ashton-beyonce-meme

Soh, Deborah
No, the Google manifesto isn't sexist or anti-diversity. It's science : https://beta.theglobeandmail.com/opinion/no-the-google-manifesto-isnt-sexist-or-anti-diversity-its-science/article35903359/?ref=http://www.theglobeandmail.com&
The left is alienating its allies by shutting down free speech: http://www.cbc.ca/news/opinion/ryerson-free-speech-1.4259360
We need to protect free speech on campus: https://beta.theglobeandmail.com/opinion/we-need-to-protect-free-speech-on-campus/article35476933/?ref=http://www.theglobeandmail.com&

Soupcoff, Marni

Canadians should be envious of the U.S.' liberal approach to controversial speech: http://nationalpost.com/opinion/marni-soupcoff-canadians-should-be-envious-of-the-u-s-liberal-approach-to-hate-speech

Universities lose the thread on reasoned discourse: http://nationalpost.com/opinion/marni-soupcoff-universities-lose-the-thread-on-reasoned-discourse

Spears, Tom

How controversial U of T prof Jordan Peterson became a lightning rod: http://ottawacitizen.com/news/local-news/how-controversial-u-of-t-prof-jordan-peterson-became-a-lightning-rod

Spegman, Abby

Evergreen settles with Weinstein, professor at center of campus protests: http://www.theolympian.com/news/local/article173710596.html

Staddon, John

Sorry, Professor, speech is not violence, even to your neurons: http://thefederalist.com/2017/07/20/sorry-professor-speech-not-violence-even-neurons/

Stafford, Tom

Female chess players outperform expectations when playing men: https://psyarxiv.com/bpy3t/

Stanger, Allison

Understanding the angry mob at Middlebury that gave me a concussion: https://www.nytimes.com/2017/03/13/opinion/understanding-the-angry-mob-that-gave-me-a-concussion.html?mcubz=3

Stevens, Sean

The Google Memo: What does the research say about gender differences?: https://heterodoxacademy.org/2017/08/10/the-google-memo-what-does-the-research-say-about-gender-differences/

Strachan, Owen

The alt-right is what happens when society marginalizes men: https://thefederalist.com/2017/03/21/alt-right-happens-society-marginalizes-men/#disqus_thread

Students for Free Expression

Facebook page: https://www.facebook.com/studentsforfreeexpression/

Sweney, Mark & Jackson, Jasper

City University students vote for campus ban on Sun, Mail, and Express: https://www.theguardian.com/media/2016/nov/18/city-university-students-vote-for-campus-ban-sun-daily-mail-express

Sweeney, Chris

How liberal professors are ruining college: http://www.bostonmagazine.com/news/article/2016/12/20/liberal-professors/

Timpf, Katherine

Campus-wide email tells white girls to stop wearing hoop earrings because it's cultural appropriation: http://www.nationalreview.com/article/445611/campus-email-white-girls-stop-wearing-hoop-earrings-cultural-appropriation

Todd, Douglas

Men do well in science and tech, but lag everywhere else: http://vancouversun.com/opinion/columnists/douglas-todd-men-do-well-in-science-and-tech-but-lag-elsewhere

Top moral thinkers defend free speech in UBC clash: http://vancouversun.com/opinion/columnists/douglas-todd-top-moral-thinkers-defend-free-speech-in-ubc-clash

Turner, Camilla

Whooping should be banned because it excludes deaf people, National Union of Students say: http://www.telegraph.co.uk/education/2017/04/27/whooping-should-banned-beause-excludes-deaf-people-nation-union/

University of Chicago Faculty

Letter: Faculty respond to Ellison with a letter of their own: https://www.chicagomaroon.com/article/2016/9/13/letter-faculty-respond-ellison-letter/

Urback, Robyn

A truly feminist government would consider the plight of indigenous men: http://www.cbc.ca/news/opinion/mmiw-mandate-urback-1.3888162

Van Geyn, Christine

http://www.huffingtonpost.ca/christine-van-geyn/political-correctness-campus-canada_b_13280954.html

Varkey Foundation (Generation Z: Global Citizenship Survey that is cited in Economist article)
https://www.varkeyfoundation.org/generation-z-global-citizenship-survey

Villasenor, John
Views among college students regarding the First Amendment: Results from a new survey: https://www.brookings.edu/blog/fixgov/2017/09/18/views-among-college-students-regarding-the-first-amendment-results-from-a-new-survey/

Vivanco, Leonor & Rhodes, Dawn
U. of C. tells incoming freshman it does not support 'trigger warnings' or 'safe spaces': http://www.chicagotribune.com/news/local/breaking/ct-university-of-chicago-safe-spaces-letter-met-20160825-story.html

Volokh, Eugene
'Professor told he's not safe on campus after college protests' at Evergreen State College (Washington): https://www.washingtonpost.com/news/volokh-conspiracy/wp/2017/05/26/professor-told-hes-not-safe-on-campus-after-college-protests-at-evergreen-state-university-washington/?utm_term=.0320b9ba137c

We The Internet [YouTube page]
The following two clips were made by filmmaker Rob Montz. These clips are of professional quality and appear to be accurate. I first learned about Ruth Simmons in these documentaries. They also cover the controversy over Halloween costumes that took place at Yale in 2015, and the aftermath of that controvery.

Silence U: Is the university killing free speech and open debate?: https://www.youtube.com/watch?v=x5uaVFfX3AQ
Silence U Part 2: What has Yale become?: https://www.youtube.com/watch?v=xK4MBzp5YwM

Weinstein, Bret
Interview with Dave Rubin (The Rubin Report): https://www.youtube.com/watch?v=-fEAPcgxnyY
Interview with Joe Rogan (Joe Rogan Experience): https://www.youtube.com/watch?v=xq4Y87idawk
The campus mob came for me – and You, Professor, could be next: https://www.wsj.com/articles/the-campus-mob-came-for-meand-you-professor-could-be-next-1496187482

Weis, Bari

When the left turns on its own: https://www.nytimes.com/2017/06/01/opinion/when-the-left-turns-on-its-own.html?mcubz=3

Wente, Margaret

Do women really have it better in Sweden?: https://www.theglobeandmail.com/opinion/do-women-really-have-it-better-in-sweden/article15552596/?arc404=true

Liberals' reverse discrimination comes at a cost: https://beta.theglobeandmail.com/opinion/canadas-war-against-merit-marches-on/article35261591/?ref=http://www.theglobeandmail.com&

Why campuses are ditching free speech: https://beta.theglobeandmail.com/opinion/why-campuses-are-ditching-free-speech/article34356708/?ref=http://www.theglobeandmail.com&

Wild Smile [YouTube Channel]

This channel contains, among other topics, footage from the protests at Evergreen State College. Given that it's someone's personal channel, the commentary must be approached with caution.

Evergreen State College closes for a day because of 'safety concerns': https://www.youtube.com/watch?v=jDmrHUf466k

Evergreen State College President is grateful for the 'passion and courage' of the Black Power protestors: https://www.youtube.com/watch?v=Z5cmnJknin0

Evergreen State College protestors demand no homework: https://www.youtube.com/watch?v=JPZ8SXQBqvg

Lawmakers vote to defund Evergreen State College after racially charged protests: https://www.youtube.com/watch?v=z-ALlQde-fs

Professor told by police that he isn't safe on campus after he opposed 'no whites day': https://www.youtube.com/watch?v=bhk9Ehe4wg8

Willinger, Jeremy

The opening of the liberal mind: WSJ op-ed by Wesleyan President Michael S. Roth: https://heterodoxacademy.org/2017/05/11/the-opening-of-the-liberal-mind-wsj-op-ed-by-wesleyan-president-michael-s-roth/

Williams, Wendy M. & Ceci, Stephen J.

Wiliams, W.M., & Ceci, S.J. (2015). National hiring experiments reveal 2:1 preference for women on STEM tenure track. *Proceedings of the National Academy of Sciences of the United States of America, 112,* 5360-5365. doi: 10.1073/pnas.1418878112

Wood, Zachary

https://heterodoxacademy.org/2017/06/23/zachary-wood-senate-testimony-on-free-speech/

Woodson, Robert L.

When student activists turn to violence: http://www.washingtontimes.com/news/2017/jul/4/civil-rights-movement-legacy-undermined-by-violent/

Yamato, Jen

Meet the black blues musician who befriended the KKK: http://www.thedailybeast.com/meet-the-black-blues-musician-who-befriended-the-kkk

Yorke, Harry

University professors afraid to teach controversial subjects for fear of being sacked, conference hears: http://www.telegraph.co.uk/education/2017/06/29/university-professors-afraid-teach-controversial-subjects-fear/

Zimmerman, Michael

The Evergreen State College implosion: Are there lessons to be learned?: http://www.huffingtonpost.com/entry/the-evergreen-state-college-implosion-are-there-lessons_us_5959507ee4b0f078efd98b0e?ncid=engmodushpmg00000004

The Evergreen State College: Is speaking with Tucker Carlson a punishable offence? http://www.huffingtonpost.com/entry/596318a5e4b0cf3c8e8d59fc

Made in United States
North Haven, CT
25 July 2023

39495964R00104